Turning Forty

Also, by Mitch Rubman

Fiction, screenplays

The Red Apartment
Rock Stars in Space
Escape From Lima
The Maelstrom Whirlpool
The Meter Maid
Don Juan and Jacques Casanova
King Arthur's Court, a lover's tale
My Uncle Z

NONFICTION

The Hollywood Tutor's American English Books one and two

The Hollywood Tutor's 2021 & 2022 U.S Citizenship and Immigration Services Interview and Naturalization Exam Study Guide

The Hollywood Tutor's Everyday American Dialogues and Brilliant Conversations

Don Juan's illustrated manual to women

Turning Forty

Mitch Rubman, M.A.

Dedicated to all of us who are getting older, Congratulations. Enjoy.

To family and friends forever forty.

Turning Forty

ISBN:978-1-7333110-5-2

Contents

Introduction

      This book is filled with love, romance, and sex. Inside the mind of a single, turning forty male. You could say that it's all about sex. Honestly, that's what it's about. It doesn't matter that I'm pursuing a master's degree in clinical psychology or that I work for several different internet companies.

I return to my childhood home and take you with me. I go inside strip clubs and move from Hollywood to NYC and back.

There are brief reviews of receiving supervision as a clinical therapist—a quick visit to the existential class, as well as a discussion of couples' therapy.

There are on /off romances and all that follows that.

Back to the Club to retrieve the old family photos.

Observe clinical interactions with borderline clients. When clients took naps, they missed their appointments.

Seeking peace. From Burbank.

Imminent truths chasing pink satin illusions.

TURNING FORTY

Chapter 1 The start

I wish that I had the happiest story to tell you about turning forty, but this is the story. What kind of insane lives do we all lead here in LA?

I never really thought of turning forty until I was close. It seems to creep up on you, and then you are there. But before that happens, you might experience more than you ever thought. And that is turning forty. That is the point in one's life when all one's wildest fantasies come true. I never really thought about thirty much, except that it meant something big, and now, well, forty; that was enormous. I always thought that my life was every day until I started to describe it. It is that everyone in LA is crazy. I do not know, but I tried to find out. My insanity was generated from a mixture of too much TV, caffeine, and not enough sex.

I cannot tell you how much I miss the occasional rainstorm, because here in Los Angeles, it never rains. It is hot. That is my summation, hot. And this is my hot story of life in LA. The life of a 40-year-old, looking at it through the eyes of myself: Marty Lovett. Someone who has spent the last fourteen years right here in LA, transitioning from acting to writing to becoming a therapist, at least in the process of studying to be one. Whatever is going on in Marty's life, will we witness it? Therefore, the team does not need to read further. This is inside Marty's mind, a place that few have gone to, and a place that fills with all sorts of strange occurrences. But there is also romance, love, and lust in Marty's life. Ok, so I am Marty.

I woke up one day and realized that I was turning forty, and that's when I freaked out, as expected. I decided that instead of just getting therapy, shock therapy, or the rack, I would enroll in the clinical psychology program at Antioch. That should help me to keep up with all the insanity that was going on. I was dealing with real life, not some happy story, but one of mysteries and intrigue- at least it was a mystery to me.

Well, I was right, up to the point where I had to deal with a whole new type of insanity, and patience. I had been dealing with my mother; sometimes these things happen in life. That is where the story begins.

It was during that period of my life when I would often find myself returning to New York to check on my mom. She had suffered two broken hips and was now staying at a nursing home in Far Rockaway.

No matter what I do in the present, I am constantly reminded of this pain; seeing my parents' age rapidly, and then: what is next?

I want to provide some background information. That is, some chapters of key moments in the last ten years.

I would have thought that by now, I would already be a successful actor. I tried to get that going, but it seemed to come and go. I was hit for a few minutes and then languished in stillness. I was able to do some surprisingly good plays; maybe five or six. But then suddenly, I think I got nervous and stopped and decided to go back to school to study psychology. I thought I was going crazy. All my crazy Internet jobs expanded that.

Work: Over the last ten years, I have held numerous jobs, but I have yet to achieve any significant successes, and I still lack a genuine sense of accomplishment. It's as if I hadn't put anything together. The most together thing is my car. I got it for my thirty-fifth birthday. It was beautiful—I still have it, a 1987 BMW L6. L stands for lots of cash because that is what you'll need to keep it going. This is one of those big two-door

Beemers that were built when people wanted cars filled with leather. This car is like being inside a cow; everything is leather.

The following subject is the story of sharks in Los Angeles - this is a significant story. Sharks, okay, some people might say that I'm obsessed with sharks. I would say "no way" just because I have built three different shark sculptures, and the last one was nine and a half feet long, does not mean anything.

After getting fired from the TV show EXTRA, I decided to build a nine-and-a-half-foot shark. This could be seen as a metaphor for my life. Some people might say that I am mad--but no, I'm just an artist having fun. The shark is like a guard dog, sitting by my window with its large teeth staring at the street life. My friends were over the other day. It's incredible how, after a while, people get used to it. I made it to scale (hey, there's a little shark humor there.)

I had a dream one night about sharks. I dreamt it was blood red, so when I awoke, I was going to paint it entirely red, but I figured it would scare me too much, so I just painted the tip of one fin. Now, whenever people see the shark in shows, they ask me about the red fin.

I am from Bayside, Queens. Pause. Deep breathe. The house, my parents' apartment, was a fantastic adventure in collecting. There was more stuff in just one room than most people had in their whole place. We will address that later.

What about relationships, you ask? Well, you are in luck, because I should have known that the relationship wasn't good. My girlfriend bought the book "Cunt" over the weekend. It is even worse. We broke up at the therapist's office. This meant that I had to pay to end the relationship. I'm sick of it, I thought to myself. Sick of what? Sick of it all. So, there I was back to where I started, only ten months later. Abby and I spent the weekend together. We even had sex twice or maybe four times. But there was something weird, in the middle of this hot sex, she went to the bathroom. Not to take a piss. Couldn't she have waited a little longer?

So, what was it like turning forty? Well, it was as if I thought I only had half my life left, and that would be a good life. I mean that I can live to 100, but with all these lattes and stressful moments, I have to admit I've had my doubts.

I wish I had some better insight into women at this point in my life, but all I can think of is the chase.

I was in the middle of breaking up with the babe, and it was hard to sleep. Too much caffeine and too much thinking of her. So, it's six am and I feel just a little better than shit, but not much. I had spent most of the night going through the whole thing in my head, and in the end, all I could say to myself was that she was the psycho. I mean, when in doubt, it's got to be her.

I had found a little love note on my printer when I got home. It said 'sweet dreams' with 'big X and OS' written all over it. Sounds loving? Doesn't it? Ok, so that was how she was. I took it out of the printer, looked at it for a moment, and then threw it out. I still miss her.

What do you do with those remnants of relationships that are scattered all around the apartment? Toss it. I found photos of her on my desk. Something that she never did. That is, I put pictures of myself on her desk. I should have known. If they don't put a photo of you on their desk, it's not love. That could be the deciding factor. I even have those little stickers of us as a Japanese couple, the kind where hearts surround our faces.

I gather up all our old pictures and put them in a box. This is the nice me, the other part just wanted to burn them. To get the fire going, say a little incantation and toss them into the flames. But I resisted the voodoo temptation, at least for now.

It was almost time to see the shrink. I won't say his name, but he is ancient and distinguished-looking, something everyone should look for in a shrink. I think he knew Sigmund Freud, but I'm not sure. His office was filled with little fetishes, masks, and dark wood paneling. It made me think that I was sitting in an office somewhere in East Africa.

One of my favorite places is King's Road Café, where I sit outside and suck down lattes and vitamins, the breakfast of champions. A beautiful woman walks over to me and comments on my laptop. Ahha... engaged in conversation, and so early in the morning. We somehow discuss the worst things that have happened to each of us, covering nine topics. I ask her what's the worst thing, and she describes her cat, Myrtle, being eaten by a coyote and getting thrown out of her apartment. She looks at her tall, slender body reflection in the window. She takes the rubber band out of her hair, letting it flow down her shoulders. Does she do this for me? Who knows? She also mentions her two jaw surgeries. I don't ask her why. But you know she is wearing braces. She had the cute look of a woman in her twenties wearing braces. A warm, friendly smile. It was just a little after 7 a.m. She is a hard worker—the caffeine from the latte races through my body. I take a deep breath.

Twenty minutes till shrink time. It's weird seeing one therapist at night, then going to another in the morning. Boy, my life must be wildly fucked up. But I'm only going to be forty. It hasn't even been enough time to be that fucked up.

It is the first full day of spring. What a happy occasion. The air is a little warmer and a bit more inviting. You might not think that was necessary in LA, but it does get cold: in the deep 40s. There is that number again. I shall have to do some research

13

on images of forty and see what comes up. I can only think of forty days and forty nights. Well, it's off to the shrink.

Okay, so I just got off the phone with the other Shrink, well, she's not a Shrink, but rather a Doctor of Psychology. In any case, she reminded me that my ex had many borderline features. And for you out there who don't know what a borderline is, look around. You know, all those psycho girlfriends out there that I have gone out with, the ones that love you one minute and hate you the next. There they go. They are the ones with feelings of intense love and hate, and boy, will they drive you crazy. There's no gray area in their menu; it's either black or white, and that's it.

No wonder I left without my stuff at her house. She would have felt crushed if I had abandoned her. I wonder if she has someone else in mind for me. There's nothing I could do or say.

I went to the shrine this morning. The old crow didn't offer any insight into my dilemma, except perhaps to remind me that there are degrees of commitment one can have. That reminds me of another thing a psychologist once said to me: that I confuse intensity with commitment in a relationship. How's that for an idea?

Oh, so you think things are over. Come on now, think again. I'm sitting at home wondering what to do next, and I remember that this new girl's phone number is in my bag. So, I start to call her when there's an incoming call, then my cell phone rings, and then Patti, the girl I met, picks up... I have hardly enough time when I call to wait for her. Just remember, she doesn't even know who I am. I had just enough time to say Hold on.

So, then I find out that it's my good friend, with an emphasis on 'friend,' Tess, on the other line. So, I told her I would call her back, then I looked at the cell and saw it was

TURNING FORTY

Kyra, Mucci's girlfriend's sister. I turned the cell off and then clicked back to Patti. This all happens within seconds. Patti says she is on the other line with her mother and asks if I can call her back in fifteen minutes. It's early, so I say OK and hang up. Wow, that was a rapid round of calls. Then, of course, Abby calls, well, here we go.

I recall having just read that a few minutes earlier, which made me feel borderline abandoned. So, there I am on the phone for an hour with Abby. She tells me her pilot light has gone off. I offer to light it for her, a pretty good metaphor. What the fuck does she want? I offer to take her with me again to Vegas and get married to Elvis, but that doesn't go over well. It's hard to talk to her. I mean, she had just totally fucked me over the night before, so naturally, I'm a little cautious.

Abby sounds so convincing that I start to pack while talking to her on the phone. I have an interview tomorrow so that I will need a suit. Piece by piece, I get the outfit together. However, after speaking with her for forty minutes, I realized the conversation was going downhill. I do not want to go over there. She is all over the place. Perhaps if I hadn't minded her giving me the boot the night before, I might have shown up. But I still felt burned-- not to mention what the two shrinks would say.

But you know how exes can be, and by the next night, I had given up. So, I spent the night at her house, and yes... we had sex. I wasn't planning it, but it happened. This is how it all went down. Abby called me a couple of times. We played one of those awful phone tag games, you know, on and off phone calls all day. This added to the tension, as everything was already tense due to electronic communication. Finally, we spoke and agreed to see an Art show later that night. Then, as I drive home through that giant parking lot, they call the 101, and suddenly my cell rings. Abby has a sweet voice, you know, the kind that makes it seem like everything is going to be wonderful. She wanted me to come over-over-I tried to resist, but what could I do? Before I knew it, I was in bed with her.

What happened? Abby is one of those women who can be very alluring in moments of need. It started when I was at the door kissing her. It was one of those sweet embraces that left one wanting more. But I could still feel the pain from the night before. The abandonment of being told that she didn't want to be in a relationship with me. How do I correct that? That was juxtaposed with my own need to be needed. How fucked up, the Borderline and the Narcissistic, a very dynamic team?

So, where did we go from there? Well…follow this. After the whole breakup episode at the therapist, we tried to get back together.

I plead with Abby to get back together. I want her to say that we are back together. She, of course, does not want to say anything of the sort. But after a few hours, she gives up and reluctantly does. It was a bittersweet victory. I don't know what to do or say. But I do have the feeling that I made a big mistake. We spent the entire night of Thursday renegotiating the terms. She wants to start again. I want to get back together. It becomes very clear after a while that she feels abandoned. So now she is chasing me. And nothing is scarier than being chased by a woman.

That's not the way it's supposed to be. Men chase women, end of story. Having her chase me threw me off, and she knew it. Which, of course, made everything harder. It wasn't fun anymore. I was hunting, but what could I do? I mean, I had spent so much time chasing her that I felt embarrassed by it all, but things got better.

In the therapist's office, she said she didn't want to be in a relationship. Now, she wants to be in one, and she is willing to

16

do whatever it takes to achieve this goal. So, we started with oral sex every day, then moved to cooking dinners twice a week. She even started to figure out a timetable for having the three children I wanted.

Chapter 2 Future Vision

My future vision: I am in my beautiful beach house in Malibu. Abby and I have three kids, two girls and a boy. The house is filled with happiness and laughter. I walked downstairs and said hello to Abby. It is a beautiful, warm kiss. I hold her in my arms, and the time seems endless. I have been working on my next screenplay, and I sit downstairs overlooking the ocean and read through the first draft. I get up, take a walk onto the porch, and take a deep breath of air. Our children are home. It is Saturday, so they came out to join me. Abby comes outside, and we comment on how beautiful the ocean is. The birds are singing, and we are all laughing. The phone rang and we were invited over to a friend's for dinner. We arranged for a babysitter. The children take one of those afternoon naps, and Abby and I sneak upstairs and have sex with the warm wind blowing into the bedroom.

I read that to her on Thursday night, two nights after the session. I thought that all the talk about the kids would scare the shit out of her. Instead, it made her want me even more. She showed me her diary—something she hadn't done in the 12 months that we had gone out. She had worked out a complete timetable for getting engaged, getting married, having children, and everything in between. Now that scared the crap out of me. There it was in ink, in her diary, the whole master plan for happiness, success, and prosperity for the two of us. So, what was the problem? It was a week late, that's all. I think well... I don't know. But when I was pursuing her, I would have agreed to anything. Of course, I wanted to get married to Elvis, but otherwise, the kids and the house in Malibu were perfect for me.

Chapter 3 The Last Night

Friday night was to be our last night together. I think that in life, sometimes we schedule things in advance, with the result that events often follow a predetermined path. Friday night, I had planned to have dinner with Gail, an old friend of mine. Gail was a very aware individual and had known me since I moved to Los Angeles, about 12 years ago. Gail and I therefore had a lot of history together, so I could open up to her about what was going on in my life. Gail had also been my acting teacher, so I had shown her all my sides. Our conversation was over dinner at a local restaurant.

It began with simply discussing what was happening. However, the larger context was about being fully and completely who you are in life and expressing yourself authentically. We also discussed the people in our lives, how we tolerate specific individuals based on some childhood memories. I began to realize that I was dating my sister. Fuck, think about that dysfunction for a moment. Dating my sister. And I hated my sister. I was brought up in one of those very hostile situations that leave one wondering what a normal person is like. I always made the analogy that I felt like I was brought up in the Munsters' house, and I was the normal one.

Gail and I discussed my relationship extensively, and at the end, I knew what I had to do. I wasn't in love with Abby, and the worst part was that she wasn't in love with me.

I think we both knew that. And that was hard. When I left the restaurant, I knew that I had another problem. I was supposed to meet her later at my place. Bad choice for breaking up with someone. Either do it at a restaurant or her house. This way, you can get your stuff and take off, and she can stay home and cry. Never do it at your place, or you'll have what I had: a crying girlfriend all night.

Add to those fears of being killed or castrated in the middle of the night, and that equals a very unpleasant sleep. But there was nothing I could do. I couldn't say, 'Don't come over,' because I would undoubtedly have to explain that, and that wouldn't be easy over a cell phone. So, all I could do was try not to discuss anything at all. But I knew I would never be that lucky. Abby called me around ten pm just after I had said good-bye to Gail.

I planned to meet Tyler, another old friend of mine, occasionally, and meet Abby around eleven, which is a busy time. Abby, in turn, wanted to visit a friend of hers and then come over to my place. But you know how it is once you've decided to end something; it's tough not to let it slip out in the context of any conversation. Well, as soon as I spoke to Abby, it became apparent that something was amiss. I could barely contain my anger that had arisen after my talk with Gail. It was frustration and fear. Abby could smell it.

The conversation was tense. I was also looking for a parking spot to meet Tyler at Canter's. Canters is an old-world Jewish deli that was very happening. It became a nightmare trying to find a parking spot. So, in the middle of driving around and around, I had to hide all the other stuff that was going on. Not easy. And when I hung up, I knew that I had begun the process of breaking up.

Canters is also a place where you might run into people you know, and sure enough, a minute after the door, I could hear someone yelling my name. I looked up and there in the first booth was the Doc, or Bob as his friends call him. I need to take a minute to describe Bob since he always appears either the day before or the day after I break up with someone. Very odd. But I didn't think of that when I saw him; instead, I looked at the beautiful 18-year-old he was with. Bob is a reconstructive surgeon.

What else can I say except that his house is the size of a small stadium at the top of a hill in the valley? So, he has it all. Why he would be sitting at Canter's and having dessert is quite amusing. But there he was, looking quite happy with himself. After a few brief one-liners, he introduced himself as a Sturgeon. I added, "You kids have fun," and moved over to sit with Tyler to discuss how life had wronged us both.

Tyler is a director and one of those rare breeds of artists who manage to avoid a day job yet remain off the streets. That always amazed me. We had had a few falling outs, but we were joined in our fight against the establishment. He showed me a letter that he had written regarding a radio station that had switched formats. He was earnest about this. I was, well, not interested at all and was amused at how involved he had become. I assured myself that he was a radical deep at heart and that the country needed him. Of course, the real context was regarding Abby and when I was going to meet her. I kept thinking to myself that she was already pissed. How could I break up with her tonight? The minutes passed very slowly.

When I left the restaurant, it was elevenish, and I got home and waited. There's nothing worse. She was at a friend's house, a guy named Bill. I called her at midnight, but of course she wasn't answering her cell, or it was out of range. So, I waited. Then, at midnight, I left a message on her home machine. She called twenty minutes later. And asked if I wanted her to come over. "Yes, of course." Was that the right thing to say, I wondered? But there was little that I could do. I had no resistance over the phone.

When she finally arrived, she called me from the parking lot, and I walked over and back with her. I tried to see her as a friend, so that I wouldn't play with my hands too quickly. I just needed to get her into my apartment and go to sleep promptly. But everything was all fucked up. Now it was so late that there would be little time tonight or in the morning.

So, I had to trust that the universe would work everything out.

When we arrived at the apartment, everything proceeded at a normal pace, and before long, we were in bed. Of course, it was almost one AM. Not an ideal time to start anything. That is, unless it's hot sex, something that we had not been doing either. So, the conversation went from "how are you feeling?" to "how am I feeling?" and then it started to happen. You cannot keep a secret like this, and before I knew it, everything was over, and we were no longer together.

The crying went on through the night. She wanted to leave, but somehow, I couldn't send her out into the night. So, we stayed in bed. I admit I don't know what I'm doing. That is how men behave sometimes. I was rubbing her back, but my thoughts were with another woman I knew. "Shit, this sucks," I said to myself.

The night moved quickly, and it was morning before I knew it. There was no denying what I had done. I broke up with her and then slept with her. The morning had that awful feeling.

It would have been better to break up with her right before a trip out of town. Then, at least, I could have said goodbye and vanished into the night. Instead, I was left thinking of her. We then went to breakfast. This became one of those sorry morning scenes. Tragically saying goodbye. But it didn't last. When the bill came, she had forgotten her wallet. I'm sorry, but how can someone forget a wallet? It is absolutely beyond my understanding. She said it was in the car. I had a flashback to my last girlfriend who did a similar thing.

I remember it as if it were yesterday. We were eating at this Spanish restaurant in San Diego, where she lived. After the whole tragic breakup moment, the bill came, and she said that she wanted to pay, but she had forgotten her wallet. I just laughed and paid the bill, "but I wanted to pay," she exclaimed, whatever. I'm sorry, am I just cheap?

Abby had mysteriously left her eyeglasses at my place.   I had no stomach for staying broken up, and after a few hours, we got back together again. Okay, I'm getting a little tired of going back and forth. Let's just say that we are together--don't ask why or how or what the fuck, let's just leave it at that for the moment. Sometimes I think that since the rest of my life is so fucked up it doesn't matter. Turning forty brings weird things into my awareness.

Today is Monday, March 27, 2000. I almost wrote that it was September, which shows how fuckin' crazy I am right now. I used to say that Mondays were Med school Mondays, and people would ask," Med school Mondays, what does that mean?" It means that had I gone to med school, I wouldn't be at this lousy fuckin' job right now. Some Mondays, I would call one of those medical schools in the Caribbean — those that teach medicine in Spanish — and you don't have to be pre-med. You don't need to have taken Organic Chemistry; you must want to live in the Caribbean, Mexico, or Granada, and there you are. Of course, you do have to have plenty of cash or just enough credit to take out enormous loans to cover you. Med school Monday. If only I had gone to medical school, I would be living like my friend the doctor, in a mansion with some zippy nineteen-year-old. Fuck, Med school Monday, how depressing. Just a reminder, Marty, of our misspent youth.

TURNING FORTY

So, where am I working right now? Like all the other losers in the country, at some fuckin' Internet company. I seem to have found the only Internet Company that doesn't have some innovative plan to make all its employees millionaires. Did I pick the only company that doesn't have an IPO plan, or what? However, the amusing thing is that I'm earning more money than I've ever made at any sales job, and I haven't sold anything in nine months. Funny, huh? Yeah, just enough to drive anyone fuckin' crazy.

So, I spend the days sitting at my computer, staring at the screen and talking to the two girls who happen to be within my scope of influence. It must be my karma with women: that I would be sitting right in the hub of absolute boredom and idiocy. I can't take it anymore.

What could be worse? Today, my immediate supervisor informed me that he wants to relocate me to an office on the second floor. Fuck, even worse--right across from the bathroom. I explained to him that it's awful Feng Shui. Then Anna, one of the only sexy women in the office, says to my boss and me, "Well, you don't have any plants inside your cubicle." What the fuck is that about? Is she a fuckin' expert? No, fuck her. So, I say in my most casual way, "Yeah, what about the plants growing between my toes?" Well, that breaks up the little group as she makes strange sounds and walks away. I love doing that.

Chapter 4 Lamont

Last night was the Oscars. Let me tell you how fucked up my evening was. Before the awards, which were held on a Sunday, I went to a great yoga class. It was one of Guru Singh's great Sunday seminars. The kind that leaves you with faith and hope. So, when Tyler called me after the class, I figured that I was going to have a great night. He told me about a party to which he was invited. He said that it was at a small new movie studio, and that we would be the guests of one of the individuals being honored. I should have known then that I was in trouble, but I was in that optimistic space that one finds oneself in from time to time.

I was so spaced out when I spoke to Tyler that I thought I was listening to a machine. You know, that after-yoga-class vibe. So, when I called Tyler, he started talking, and I was listening when suddenly I heard him repeat his statement. I thought the machine was repeating itself. Very odd. He said, "Do you have a pen or something to write with?" I thought I was listening to the machine. After the third time, I said, "What?" He said, "A pen, do you have a pen? I'm in a rush." It occurred to me that I was listening to Tyler live, not on tape, and not on my machine. I was surprised.

I took down the information, and he said that we would meet later at the party. "What time will you be there?" I asked. He said seven. Ok, so I got into my car and looked up the address in the Thomas guide. It was way south, as in South Central LA. You know, the place where the riots started. So, that was where I was headed. Fuckin' great. Well maybe, I thought, it's a beautiful studio undergoing urban renewal and all that shit.

TURNING FORTY

I should've known that I was in trouble when I pulled up at 6:45 and almost no one was there. The Oscars started at six, so they had already begun, and I got a parking spot right in front, another bad sign. That should have been the next clue. I stepped in and I was right. I was probably the first one. Now, for me, that's not that unusual, but not usually at an Oscar party. I was one of three white people there, and there were no giant screens.

I was wearing a very nice blue suit. They were setting up upstairs, but there was no telecast. Downstairs in the office, there was. So, I sat there with two other white folks for at least an hour and watched the show. This was fine except that we were occasionally interrupted by a gray mouse that had made the office his home. The movie fit in well with "The Green Mile," which didn't win anything.

I stayed for the entire Oscars. A few of us took a break to get some chicken upstairs as a snack. And yes, this was a very odd situation. I was probably the only young white guy in a suit in the entire place, and I would guess that there were about five hundred people, but it was fun in its way. Of course, Tyler, my good friend, never showed up. He got busy at the Writers Guild. Nice. Mental note, I'll have to repay the favor.

I haven't discussed it with my parents. My father died about four years ago. He didn't have any life insurance. My mother didn't do very well under the pressure of being alone. My legacy was a house filled with antiques that I had to clean and empty. There is very little of any significant value. But we'll get back to that later.

No, I don't want to do a bong load, I said to Dopey. How easily one's past can catch up with the present. What is up with that drug pot? I think it's one of those things that the planet produces just in case the world gets fucked up and we all want out. I believe that it soothes our pain, or rather, it temporarily eliminates the pain. I don't know, is it better to feel the pain of life, or better to have it blasted from our memory? Pot: the whole flipping country is filled with people with an addiction, and no one is addressing it, why? Cause no one wants to address the issues, whatever they might be.

I was still sleepy from the pasta I had just consumed at intermezzo. I think my spending on food today was about seventy dollars. Shit, that's a lot of fuckin' money and that's not even counting lattes.

I moved upstairs to that annoying place I call work. That place where I spend sixty hours a week. I hated that fact. All I could think about was the lousy fourteen hundred I got each week. What a motivating factor: cash. I had sold out for $1,400, and after taxes, well, it's even worse. Don't get me wrong, that is a lot of money, not in terms of becoming a millionaire, but in terms of the country, it's a lot.

They moved me upstairs, probably so they could check up on the slacking off that I did every day. Anyway, the only reason I agreed was that my cubicle was right across from Romano, a tall blonde Czech. She sits across from me. Yesterday I accidentally saw her...well, what do you think? She had been wearing a short skirt, and well, that's how it goes. Today she wore pants. But we went out for coffee anyway. I just wanted to grab her. I think I did well. She needs a visa, so of course I offered to marry her. The company can send us to Hawaii for their honeymoon.

I still don't know what to do about Abby. I just finished reading the article on attachment theory that the new shrink had given me. What the fuck. So, it all has to do with the first year and how your mother treated you. I'm not too sure about my mom. However, there is the fact that my sister was fourteen months older than I, so she spent her first year with my mom pregnant. That might have been tough.

Well, it's on, it's off, and it's Saturday morning now. I managed to get a slight reprieve from spending Friday night with her. We did talk on the phone. She called me before I went out. It was Stinky Doyle's birthday, and we celebrated. The party was at Lamont's. Now, I don't recall if I have or haven't described Lamont yet, but let me give it a shot here. He was the African American side of our group.

Lamont's apartment was crammed with as much stuff as possible without being utterly bizarre-looking, but it was close. Mucci & Scott were inside Lamont's bedroom. Mucci was amazed at what he found when he opened each drawer. The haberdashery, the clocks that had the wrong time, the women's mink stole in the corner. Wait… a mink stole, what was that? The discussion regarding the mink lasted a long time. It made no sense, and we never thought even to ask why he had a mink stole neatly placed in the corner.

Doyle's mom was there, and when the guys, or crew, or thugs, as we affectionately put it, decided to smoke a joint, Doyle made sure to mention that they invited his mother. "Yeah, she was the first one I smoked with," he claimed. Whatever, his mother? Never mind. The guys spent the next half hour trying to figure out how to get some water delivered. Pellegrino or Perrier. They called pink dot and Bogies, and, in the end, they decided to walk over to Ralph's to pick up four bottles of Pellegrino. When they got back, we met in Lamont's kitchen. It was Pellegrino for everyone. Only it wasn't that ice cold that we had all envisioned. "It's never as good as you think," I said to rune. That's life. Scott was debating life with Mucci. I sat back and listened.

TURNING FORTY

Have you heard the story about the duke? Duke, that is Duke Ellington, had a personal manager who paid all his bills. He didn't want it to conflict with his music.

The party ended around 1:30 a.m., so I decided to go to my new hangout, the strip club. Now that I am turning forty, this suddenly seemed like a logical place to go. I stopped at the Coronet Bar and had a scotch on the rocks, collected as many singles as I could, and I was off.

The Strip club is heaven at times. Well, maybe not heaven, but most certainly a perfect dream. Naked and semi-naked women walking around. This was a whole nudity place, no alcohol. And I had been there a bunch of times, so the girls started to recognize me and became a lot nicer. Not that they gave me head in the bathroom, but there was that overall effect of familiarity. Some of them I knew by name.

Cheyenne and I had bonded. She was from the East Coast and had a grandmother in Great Neck, near where my aunt lived. At one point, we were discussing Great Neck, and she mentioned Bruce's, a deli I had visited many times. I laughed and said to myself, "I feel connected"-she was semi-clad when she said that.

So, I walked into the club and was greeted with the kind of familiarity that might scare some people, but only encouraged me. I sat down and watched the girls slowly reveal all their business, and I mean all. Iris was my favorite. She was tall, blonde, thin, and friendly. I would sit, and she would lean over the edge and brush her hair and hands over my body. Well, at least over my head. That was heavenly, and for a moment, I almost forgot that I had to keep giving her money. Who cares? She was sweet, and she smiled, and there were no problems between us—just love. Ok, maybe not love, but I was happy for the moment. I stayed at the club until almost four am and then realized that I couldn't even keep my eyes open long enough to look at all the T and A that were surrounding me. It was time to go.

I love getting home at four am. This is something exciting for me. It makes me feel like I am living on the edge. And I always fall asleep right away. In the morning, I found myself at King's Road, a place where coffee has a new meaning. It means wake the fuck up. Strong coffee.

Chapter 5 Flamenco

I am sitting in the living room and on my bed right now, right at this very moment, there are two very hot babes. I want to say that I slept with both of them, but you know that's not true. One of them, Marena, is from Barcelona. She is 5 feet eight inches or 1.5 meters, as she would say. The other woman is Karina, Mucci's girlfriend, Claudia's older sister. She is soon to be a lawyer, and in her spare time, she is a flamenco dancer. Great body. We spend quite a bit of time looking at her toes. The ingrown one, that is. How did I get so lucky? Well, I slept on the couch anyway. But the girls were coming up from San Diego, a reference point for gorgeous women, and they needed a place to stay, so naturally I offered them my humble abode.

I think Marena liked the shark hanging in the living room. She went over and gave it a pet. If only I were that shark, how happy I might be. They are quietly sleeping in my bed now. I am very tempted to make myself a sandwich, or should I say make myself into a sandwich.

Other than that, last night had its usual difficulties. It was April fool's day. I went over to Noshi to get some sushi and met some girls. Her name is Lizzie. She is the manicurist to the stars. She was very lovely, and we talked over spicy tuna and eel. She even has an agent. Imagine that. She is, of course, also an actress. Only in Los Angeles could a manicurist have an agent.

Today could be my last rendezvous with Abby for a while. Next week school starts again. Did I even mention that I am getting a master's degree in clinical psychology? Is that not surprising? I mean, who needs it more than me? Well, school starts on Monday, so I'll be getting busy. So, the fact that I do not call her or go over to her house won't seem that obvious.

On Wednesday, I am going to Vegas with the company. Well, just with my boss. Someone asked me last night how I liked my job. I said, "it sucks, End of story." I have to get a writing job, or an acting career, or a job as a painter, or a job working with elephants in therapy. Just something using my creative juices. That's the problem: when you're Turning Forty, you realize that life isn't forever and that if I died tomorrow, I would have left nothing for posterity, humanity, or society, whichever comes first.

Abby and I were on and off again, and still, I didn't know what to do. It was tearing me apart. I had a vision of myself as a knight in the middle, battling on all sides, with the floor below me hot and shifting up and down. So, there I was on a heated floor doing the dance and boy did it suck. Not a great image for one's life.

How was work? Well, I was so upset that I almost quit my lousy $1,400-a-week job. What could be more pathetic? I don't know, perhaps staying at a job that sucked. Whatever. I came home to find a rejection letter from UCLA's film school, the screenwriting program.

TURNING FORTY

I am at Abby's, and she is in the living room with Ruth, the friend who introduced us. I will have to pick up the discussion regarding Ruth later. For the time being, I am reading the Yalom book on group therapy. It is talking about the here and now. When in doubt, that is the place to start with. Go back here and now. I won't bore you with any more antics of Abby and me. We seem to be on right now. Here and now.

Well, here I am at the Urth Café. This must be one of the most popular places to eat in Melrose. It is located next to the Bodhi Tree bookstore. Let me demonstrate the Here and Now by trying to be a little more present in the moment. I feel like I'm going to explode. Now, is that a metaphor? Or am I just really bloated? How attractive, in any case, I would like to explode. Let me explore that concept for a moment. What would that look like? Not good.

My boss asked me if I had reached a decision. Decision? As if I could make one. Shit, all I could think about was how much I hated the job and wanted to quit.

It was Friday, that day when the working class gives thanks for only a 5-day work week. Aren't we lucky? I had a moment of fun at work. I have to go to lunch with Cynthia. One of those quirky late twenty-year-olds who laughs at everything, as if things were going to be just fine in a later life. It was fun after those two sake shooters. That always helps. I also received a call back from a place regarding a job. This was a real winner: soliciting funds from people for film projects. It sounded a little like a scam, but not entirely a bad thing.

I never took the job. I thought about having to work for no money and losing interest. Fuck it. I could give a shit. All I wanted to do was act and not get old; forty looked ancient. I was miserable everywhere I turned in my life, and my relationship echoed the feelings.

TURNING FORTY

Abby and I celebrated our first anniversary, and it was very bittersweet. I had wanted to break up all day, and sure enough, I was very close, except that I had therapy that day. Therapy, even being a "would-be therapist," didn't help. I approached Selma with an open mind, and sure enough, by the end of the session, I was convinced that things would be okay. What did I know?

I met Abby at the Sawtelle Kitchen, a restaurant that was half Chinese and half Japanese, and something else in between. I just got her a card. I wanted to get her an engagement ring, but she said no. I was upset and confused. We had talked the night before. Never talk to a girl about getting her a present. It only ruins the moment. That's for sure. She said she was getting me a candle. How fuckin' cheap is that? She is a millionaire, and she gets me a candle. Fuck her. Dinner alone costs fifty dollars. But I should have gotten her a gift. She started to cry the moment she found out that she got nothing but a card, right in the Sawtelle kitchen. That sucked. We lit her candle at the table, which was a nice gesture. So, we sat there and consumed fifty dollars' worth of fish. On the way home, I picked up a dozen roses, and that didn't help. She gets me a candle; I buy dinner and get her roses, and she barely talks to me.

We went back to her place and didn't have sex. How fuckin' pathetic. No sex. I couldn't even get laid on our anniversary. I woke up early, but she had been scheduled to go jogging in the morning with her friend, the woman who had introduced us, but she cancelled. Abby still wanted to go to yoga, and I convinced her to stay. Then what rarely ever occurs in my relationships occurred. I gave her head, she came and stopped, and didn't take care of me. I was unsatisfied. That was it. Fuck her and all her drag, as Lamont would say. I could see that I was quickly losing interest in her and all her bullshit.

The next day, she had a revelation during her therapy session: she realized how meaningful the relationship was, and she wanted to continue. Shoot it already, it's dead. Fuck, what the fuck to do? I went to work at my miserable Internet job. Fourteen hundred a week, and I still wasn't happy - what a surprise. I called my mom from work.

Chapter 6 Nursing Homes

My mother has been living in a nursing home, although you would never know it by asking her. She asked about my sister. Boy does life suck sometimes. She wanted to speak to her lovely daughter. I'm even embarrassed to describe the last few months. She was challenging to deal with, and yet I had to deal with her. My mom asked for her again and again. So, I conferred with her at the office. She wasn't home, but I did get my mom to leave her a message, and for the first time, she said that she was in a Nursing home. Hallelujah.

Then the weekend was upon me. I wanted to get stoned. Why? I don't know. I guess it probably has to do with stress. I had tried to do it earlier, but somehow it ended up happening later in the day, about an hour before I had to pick Abby up at the meditation center. What the fuck was I thinking? I had lost my mind. I walked into the lion's den. I was the only one who hadn't done the weekend retreat, and I was stoned. That sucked. I wandered around in the group, paranoid. What I didn't know was that I was the only one out of the entire group who hadn't done the retreat. Why did Abby invite me? I walked around and snacked on some food, then tried to act as normally as possible under the circumstances, but it didn't work. I felt like I was going to explode. It was one of those awful moments in one's life.

Abby and I eventually left, and then Abby got her car and took off. What a relief.

I went home to watch "The Matrix." Oh, in case you haven't seen it... he dies in the end. Let's say I am in "the matrix" and I don't know how to get out of it except for the fact that I am in it. That is a trippy movie. Makes you wonder, are we all just feeding machines or what?

I had a flashback to a dream from the other day. It was a kind of flash from Guru Singh. He had trained some comedians. I think it was a message for me to be a stand-up comedian, another dream that I have always had.

Well, last night was the final for Marty and Abby. I want to be able to say that it was one of those beautiful endings, but when does that ever happen? I found myself sitting at this awful sushi restaurant. The kind that offers discounts on sushi to attract customers. Very noisy. I wanted to break up, but I couldn't figure out how to do it.

Why do women always think that it is somehow easier for guys to break up? It isn't. I sat at the table, staring at her beautiful eyes, and I was heartbroken. I could sense what I needed to do, but I was having a hard time doing it. Before I left my apartment, I said to myself, "This is it." What the fuck is the matter with me? But as I was leaving, I took my contact lens container, just in case it wasn't the end, and we went over to her house. Besides the sushi, we had Sake and beer. Nothing like covering up your feelings. That was a mistake; now I was disconnected enough that I could end the relationship easily and without feeling, like some fuckin' zombie.

I listened to Abby talk about wanting to go out with eighteen-year-old guys, and that was enough to trigger that defensive moment when you want to say... "Well, then, go out with them and give me a fuckin' break." But I didn't. Instead, I mildly shifted the conversation to, What about us? She then said it wasn't working, and I agreed; it was over. That was it. Except that I paid the bill. She said, "I'm broke." The poor millionaire. Whatever.

We had a few moments at her car chatting and caressing. We hugged so many times that it was like we were together. I mentioned to her that when I think of breaking up, I sometimes imagine that we are travelers who had met, had an affair, and now have to go back to our respective countries. On paper it sounded good, but it sucked, and it was just another illusion. Nevertheless, we said goodbye and she drove off. I looked at her as she drove away. I turned back a few times, and then she was gone from my life, gone from all the instances we had shared. The pain began. It was still early. I knew there was only one place to go, the strip club.

Before I went into the club, it was only 7:30, I went to the Coronet bar and had a couple of beers. Two women were sitting at the bar, getting hammered. They were going to go to the show at the theatre. The one woman who sat closer to me was attractive in her 30s and had been drinking all day. She was very friendly. I smoked a cigarette, and the two women explained how they had knocked over the stirrer container. They started to laugh hysterically; it was a pretty funny routine, and I could tell that the bartender was only mildly amused. I didn't bother to take any numbers; I mean, I had just broken up. After two beers, I walked outside and called Kyra, one of my best friend's twin sisters.

When I told Kyra that she was the first person I called, she seemed slightly amused and surprised. Jokingly, I said to her that I called her because she was so sensitive. She thanked me, and that seemed to make her very happy. I had always wanted to sleep with her. She was very stacked. So, we talked for a few minutes and then we agreed to get together the next day, Sunday.

It was early when I entered the strip club. There were only two obvious losers at the number one table. The rest of the club was empty. It wasn't even eight o'clock. The big fat black bouncer was eating in the back. I walked in, sat down, and ordered two fake beers. There is no real alcohol served at the all-nude clubs, in case you didn't know. This was one of those lackluster evenings that, no matter how beautiful or sexy they are, I wasn't that interested. Call me a hopeless romantic, but I found myself missing Abby and bored at the club.

I stayed at the strip club for a couple of hours. I was distraught. There was a beautiful, dark-skinned woman who got to me. She was very sensual, not her body, which was great, but her face. A few more people were sitting around the ring, and one of the guys must have said something bad to her. The strippers love to get close. Usually I whisper into their ears, "you look wonderful tonight," or "you smell great," or "you are more beautiful each time I see you." This time I said, "You look great," and she said, "Thanks, but that other guy ruined my whole evening." As she got up to leave after her routine, she threw the two dollars back at the guy and told him he could keep it. She then stormed off. So, she'll only make $998 today. I was intrigued and started to feel protective of her. I must remember to talk about that in therapy.

I moved over to the tables by the wall and stared into space and the strippers. One of them, a new one, came over and tried to convince me to do a lap dance. It was funny to listen to her try to convince me, but no matter what, I wasn't interested. I told her that it was too much work for me. She didn't understand until I explained that the work was not jumping up and grabbing her. That was work. That was much harder than dancing on my lap. She didn't understand and walked away, annoyed.

Then Iris came over to talk with me. She was wearing these adorable blue shorts and a top with long white stockings. Very sexy. She was from Florida. We talked quite a bit before. I asked how she was doing; I knew that she lived with an out-of-work gourmet cook and was going through her stuff. I told her that I had broken up with my girlfriend. She seemed surprised that I was at a strip club. Then she got up to dance and I tipped her a few dollars as she stuck her ass in my face. How weird is that? Sometimes I should get up and dance just once to see what it is really like. After a while, I got bored and started to feel depressed. It was time to go.

I walked outside and checked my messages; sure enough, Abby had called me. I immediately called her back and left a message. Then I drove home with that feeling, feeling unsatisfied with everything. I called her when I walked in the door, but her machine picked up, so I hung up. "Braveheart" was on cable, so I had a little warfare to watch. I sent Abby an email. I was now calling her "princess Honey Bud." I just said that I missed her and that she was the best I could do.

I called Abby again, and this time she picked up. She was hanging out with Ruth, the woman whose party we first met at. The girls were bonding. I hate that. My conversations with her would have been much more effective had she been alone. I can't even remember what I said, but I'm sure it was pathetic.

I tossed it and turned out like a well-made salad. I woke up at eight thirty and called her. I woke her up. "Come on, Abby, just one more chance. Let's get a place together in Malibu." I tried to imitate the sound of the ocean on the phone. "Beautiful house on the water." Then, the call waiting interrupted the moment. "I'll call you right back," I said and went back to the ocean sounds and the fireplace in Malibu. Abby told me to take care of myself and take a bath or a shower. I started to crumble. I hope I didn't whimper. "Malibu, let's take the leap of faith." She was out. That was the end. I hung up. I contemplated taking a shower and slicing my wrists, but I had too much stuff to do. So, I went out to King's Road to have a killer café latte, death by caffeine.

Emily at King's Road was getting her braces off in two days, and she had one of those happy dispositions that remind one that even if you must work all your life, you don't have to be miserable. I loved that. She was taking care of kids on the side to make money—good candidate for a wife. I must get her number, a mental note.

I'm home, and yes, Abby did call me. So, she is sleeping with my stuffed bear. Lucky fucker. "I wish I were the bear," I said to her. "You sound good, why do you sound so good?" "You sound too good," and we went back and forth. It was one of those strained conversations. "Sex and the City" was on in the background. That is a great show, and I watched it for hours. It was hilarious talking with her about our relationship and seeing "Sex and the City" on TV at the same time.

I had another one of those celebrity dreams last night. It was with Tom Hanks. "How did you start as a comedian?" I asked him, inside his beautiful house. He said, "I papered the house and took my bows early." The subconscious is a complex entity; I'm not sure what that means. But I did feel honored to be inside his house. It was decorated in silver and was very quiet. "This is my sanctuary," he said. Then I woke up and I was in my messy one-bedroom apartment. Life can suck sometimes.

Chapter 7 New Age Love Notes

I was working at the gourmet food trade show, pitching our e-business solutions. The show featured several beautiful women serving exotic food. This was the second day. I only had four suits, and the jacket for one of them was at work, which left me with three—one of which I had worn the previous day, leaving two. The light blue suit was the one I had planned to save for wearing on Passover, leaving my father's old gray suit. I had taken it back from Bayside. Wearing my father's old suit at forty, I should just fuckin' kill myself, how pathetic. Well, at least it was clean.

I just got off the phone with Lizzie; she sounds very nice. I met her at Noshi Sushi. We spoke on the phone for 45 minutes, which was pretty good. You know you're going to get some action when they mention nudity on the first phone call. She was talking about a theatre group she had recently joined, which features a lot of nudity. Sounds fine to me, I thought.

I had a meeting with an old lawyer friend of mine, or rather, a past counsel with whom I had been in touch for the last few years. Gregg was in his forties. We hadn't talked much, but I had sent him new business cards as I moved from job to job. He was interested in the Internet for the firm and had been making a considerable effort to meet as many different people as he could. I was one of them. After about 30 minutes of business, we began discussing women. He was sharing his perspective, which was exciting to listen to. "They're all crazy," or did he say, "They're all psycho?" Wow, that was quite a bold statement. I told him about Abby, how we had been going back and forth. I didn't tell him about the orgy she had had at her house, but I tried to convey that I was thinking about marrying her. I told him she was rich, and that interested him. I suppose his wife's struggles with poverty and raising children had a lasting impact on him, as having enough money was a significant concern. Gregg and I joked about how things can get so desperate that people kill themselves or each other. Whatever. I told him about my forays into strip clubs. He would only add that they do get bored after a while.

Abby and I had been exchanging emails, a kind of new-age love note, and it was driving me crazy. You can be so personal and yet entirely disconnected; all those losers in the cyber world have cybersex. Oh yes, Gregg told me about a friend of his who would seduce women on the phone to the point that at their first meeting, they would always want to have sex.

Wednesday night was the first day of Passover—one of those Jewish holidays where the history of the past is retold amongst a festive meal. Since I had no local family of my own, I had to find a surrogate family to turn to. I had been trying to get together with this one girl from school. I wasn't sure how crazy she was, although I do have to admit that she did seem a little depressed to me. Since I had no plans for this first night of Passover, I decided to take her up on her invitation. So, I met her at her grandparents' house. I could tell that I wasn't that interested in her just by the way I only slightly cared about who I was in her family, whom I was meeting. I sat next to her and these beautiful women. All they did was complain about men. "He didn't call me, should I call him?" No. "Why was I so mean to him?" she kept asking herself. She had asked him if his Porsche was leased, if he was gay, and several other similar questions. What a surprise, he didn't call.

I slept over at Abby's: great sex. Shit, now what have I done? We were back together, or we weren't. What to do? I don't know.

It's Easter Sunday. I usually have some great sexual experiences on Easter Sunday. I am doing something wrong with my life, it sucks. School has become an albatross. I was watching a Range Rover commercial last night, and I realized that my master's degree is costing me the same price as a new Range Rover. How sick am I? Very. Life sucks and I don't know what to do. I would kill myself, but who would take care of all the stuff I have? So, I find myself once again at King's Road, my home away from home. It is one of those busy Sundays. Oh, that's right, I was going to tell you about one of my great Easter seductions. OK, here it goes.

It starts the night before, as I remember it. I was at a party at a friend's house in Boston. One of those, with not too many people and no eligible women either, is a vibe. But it was a good friend, so I decided to get drunk, not that I wouldn't have done it anyway, but it was a good excuse, nonetheless. Nothing happened, even though I do seem to recall getting some offer that if I couldn't sleep, I might be invited into this woman's bed. But it was very suspect as I recall, in any case, I had awoken early in the morning with my hard on, sleeping on the couch. It was a morning boner, and there was absolutely nothing I could do about it. I was in someone's living room, so I couldn't just jerk off, not that I do that anyway. In any case, I got up. It must have been around 9 am, and I decided to exit the couch and the morning vibe at the house to see what the universe had to offer.

I decided to go to the North End of Boston for my Easter meal. I know I'm Jewish, but it was a good excuse to eat. It was one of those ways that allowed me to feel a little warmth and enjoy lots of cheesy foods. The restaurant that I would go to was called Damore's, a lovely place to go alone. Anyway, I had some eggplant Parmesan, paid the check, and decided to hit the road. Damore's was on Salem Street, right in the heart of the North

End. It was a warm and sunny day, perfect for the occasion. I was horny, and it was Easter Sunday.

A day of funny hats and sexy dresses. I was walking in the middle of the street, something you can do without getting hit by a car in the North End, when I walked in front of this very sexy woman standing in a doorway. She had jet-black hair and beautiful green eyes. As I walked by, she asked me if I was there to see the apartment. I looked at her and thought for a moment or half a moment. I could feel myself being seduced in the moment. And before I knew what I was doing, I said yes.

I was a student at Boston University at the time, receiving a degree in Planetary and Space Sciences. In any case, I was certainly not in the market for a condominium. I wonder if Pat knew that. The apartment was located in one of those historic old Boston buildings, featuring beautiful brickwork and narrow doorways. We slowly walked up step by step through the exposed brick doorways. It was like a maze. We started to chat. She told me about the apartment, and I looked at her sexy black bra leaking through a white lace shirt. Her beautiful green eyes were mesmerizing, and all I wanted to do was grab her right on the staircase, but I resisted. We walked up to the apartment, which was on the third floor. It was a charming apartment, empty with a great view. We talked and talked, I couldn't even remember what we talked about, but each minute I got closer to her.

She was recently divorced, in her thirties, and had a killer body. We were alone in the apartment. We laughed, and I never really explained why I was there. But somehow my hands started to rub her body. I began to give her a gentle massage. I was all over her. We were on the floor grinding. It was heaven. We had just met, and I was having the time of my life. The memories of the previous party were fading, and I started to have a good time. I didn't fuck her, although later I realized that I could have. But it was wild. She gave me a lift home, and we exchanged phone numbers. For the next three months she was to be my divorcee that wore black lace that fucked the brains out of me. It was great and I was sorry when it ended. But I seem to recall that the day it ended, I met Olivia, which was another whole story. That is why I love Easter; it has a little special meaning for me, and now, I hope, for you.

Back to the present. Easter Monday would have been another boring Monday, except for the phone call I got at 1:30 a.m. from Abby, crying hysterically, as she felt her life had no meaning. She couldn't have waited until 8 am to call me? It was after she was hanging out with her girlfriends. What could I say? Sure, your life has meaning. Sure, you have friends. Sure, there is a purpose to all of this. I had my doubts, which means yeah, right. "Get up and go to work," as my dad, Sol, would say.

The height of the workday came when we sent out seven hundred emails to toy manufacturers. One of them was sent to the company where we first found the list. The owner called me and asked if we could remove the robot from his site. The Internet: the place for snaking emails and other such devious work.

It was therapy day. To summarize the session, the last thing the therapist said was, "Don't sign any leases." I had mentioned that Abby and I had attended a real estate board meeting.

One of those days.

Sometimes, Abby and I would talk about what we had done during the day. That was always hard for me. How can I communicate the absolute boredom of working for an Internet company and yet make it sound exciting? I tried to explain what I was doing. But since it was not entirely clear to me, it never really made sense.

But today there was a surprise. Abby had found the perfect color nail polish to match her new cell phone. Hey, now that was exciting—the privileged class, how I longed to have a simpler life.

Abby called and wanted to have dinner. I have this huge paper to do for school, so I tried to get out of it. It is amazing how difficult that can be. I started to feel guilty. Why? Who knows, but it set the evening off on a sour note. In any case, I stayed home and lay down on my favorite couch. It was heaven. I turned on the TV and started to relax.

The paper I was working on was about psychodrama. A subject that I should have no problems with. Isn't my life a psychodrama? After asking myself that question several times, I realized that this was my life to create. Anyway, psychodrama seems to have been popular in the past. I had obtained a list from the Internet of therapists who did psychodrama. I should explain a little about what it is. From what I understand, it is a way of combining acting and therapy. The idea is that to go deep into one's life, one has to examine one's relationships with family, and what better way to do that than by recreating not only your whole family but also a key moment of conflict from your past. Sounds entertaining?

I pulled a list of psycho dramatists from the Internet and started to call the ones in California. What I soon discovered was that it seemed like a dying art. All the therapists I spoke with were either old or no longer doing much. I got sad hearing this one woman who kept trying to sell me books. That was unusual, and it had a profound impact on me. I was not sure how to react and started to get a little depressed. I sat down and somehow pieced together a paper.

News? Well, after one year and two weeks, Abby and I finally broke up. Ok, so we did it on the phone. Were you thinking that we were already broken up? Fooled you. It was weird. She was crying and starting to talk about having a bad p.m., and before I knew it, we were talking about wanting to be with someone that we loved. I had been waiting the whole time to meet someone I loved. I couldn't agree more. That was the problem with everything. That we each wanted to find someone who had fallen in love with each one of us. Abby told me that she didn't feel loved in the world. She didn't know who loved her. She wasn't sure about her friends.

How many friends do I have? Maybe a handful. I kept trying to convince her of how great she was. She did all these wonderful things, but why wasn't I in love with her? She also tried to trick me into saying what it was that bugged me about her. I wanted to tell her that it was her use of manipulation that drove me crazy, how she kept on asking questions without giving out any information. She could keep the conversation going and make it about the other person, getting me to reveal as much as possible. I hated that kind of manipulation. I must admit it was not easy saying goodbye to her.

I told her that I might not know for a few hours how I felt. I sometimes go into shock. She started to laugh hysterically. I hated it when she did that. It went on and on. A man in shock. I suppose that's an unusual image. I didn't know what else to say or do.

I think Abby and I were left feeling that we didn't know what went wrong and didn't know what to say. That was very sad for both of us. When she described herself, I thought she sounded pretty good. I thought she sounded great. But I must realize that she left out a few things. I said that we were both difficult to get along with, and she asked me to describe what I meant by that. She sweated me. I'll miss her ball-busting.

It was my first night without her. I want to say that I did something fun and exotic, but I was busy finishing this fuckin' paper for school. I thought about going to the strip bar, but it was already after one am and my body was tired, a time to rest. I reviewed all the emails that we had sent to each other. A lot of "I love yours" and "cutie pies."

I have been working continuously on the psychodrama paper. But there is a party today with some of the local Antioch students and me. At the party, I ran into an old friend who is a yoga instructor. I must hand it to him; he seems pretty set up.

Teaching yoga, now that's what I'm going to do. Just quit all this other shit and teach yoga. Now I am a single man. But no big breaks. If only I were rich, I could make a difference.

Chapter 8 May Day

Today is Mayday; the first day of May in the year 2000. Just in case I had neglected to inform you sooner. But ultimately, it is Monday, and Monday is Med school Monday to me. I should have been a doctor. I might have been a gynecologist—that way, all day could be spent looking at women. Yes, I still haven't spoken with Abby. It's been two whole days.

There weren't many saving graces at the Internet Company where I worked, one of which was Romano, a tall blonde.
Czechoslovakian woman. Today she was wearing a long beige dress. Her nipples were popping through. All this and it's only nine thirty. She said she wanted some coffee. "Let's go," I replied. "Right now?" She said. All I wanted to do was to take her anywhere and have hot sex with her. And why not? She said that she would join me momentarily. She liked my good company. She is from another country.

TURNING FORTY

It had been a long weekend. I had written three papers and broken up with Abby. It was Monday, and my feelings were finally catching up with me. I didn't know what to do with all her sweet emails. It hurts. Shit, I hate that feeling. I think about what our house might have looked like. That sucks. I called her on my way home while driving through Topanga Canyon. I could have waited longer, but it had been two whole days. I am going to Detroit tomorrow.

So here I am in Detroit and up in the air. I called Abby from the airport, and we talked for a few minutes. It was good. Back and forth, that's how I am.

Retail slut: that's what I should be called. I visited the world headquarters of Kmart. It felt like being inside the spaceship from "Aliens." Long dark gray halls, a central atrium. Well, anyway, it would have been boring had we not met with Don, the owner of the minority-owned company we were visiting. He was one of those jolly 60-year-olds, slightly overweight and funny. He wouldn't stop laughing. Of course, I kept making jokes. He was going to give us a tour of Detroit, so I asked him if we could go ice fishing instead. Well, I thought it was funny at least. In any case, we presented this entire plan for creating TV commercials for the liquid cleaner and then directing traffic to the website we were going to build for them. We would use the money that came in to help pay for the site's construction. Kmart, shit, is this what life is about?

The hotel we stayed in was one of those cut-rate places that didn't have any shampoo or conditioner in the bathroom. I ended up using bar soap. The hilarious thing was that after we left the hotel, I looked in my bag and noticed that I had inadvertently taken the TV remote control. I shared this with the group at the office, and we all laughed. I was going to send it back, but now I'm thinking that it might be more fun to keep it.

I'm at Detroit airport right now. They have a new place to check emails, send faxes, etc., so I went in and checked the email. Not much except for the email from Victoria's Secret, but at 38 cents a minute, I kept it quick.

Yes, I miss Abby. Ok, there, I said it. It's so weird. I mean after all the shit; I still miss her. Maybe it will be different in a few days. I hope so. I had one of those pains in my heart. You know, one of those pains. In any case, I am in Detroit. Panic in Detroit.

We also went to the motorsport casino. Isn't that funny, a casino in Detroit? It had the same shadowy elements as the ones in Vegas—the smoke, the lights, the sexy looking babes walking around asking for drinks. Yes, I was up at first, then after about twenty minutes, I lost the fifty I won, and then another forty. I had one of those standard casino experiences.

So now I am missing her once again. I just went through the emails again, and, God, it's hard to read them and see the progression of the love affair we had. From "I love you" to a casual conversation. What does that all mean? I certainly don't know. I will probably download the emails at some later point, but how painful is that? But I have good news. How about a great story: fame?

We all have fifteen minutes of fame, as Andy Warhol once said, or rather, it was sixty minutes in my case.

Chapter 9 Don Juan

Years ago, when I lived in New York, I was an aspiring actor. I had one of the most bizarre experiences that has ever happened to me. I was in my tiny six hundred- and forty-five-dollar studio with no kitchen apartment when I saw an ad in the Village Voice; that very same paper that we had all heard about. In any case, I saw this ad for "Don Juan's wanted" for this interview. Not that I was serious… well maybe I was, in any case, this ad was asking for Don Juan's, so I thought to myself, "this might be fun." At the time, I was studying "Don Juan" written by Brecht and Moliere for a Directing class I was taking. That is "Bertolt Brecht" for anyone out there who hasn't heard of him. I was also reading George Bernard Shaw's "Don Juan."

So, I was thinking of "Don Juan" a lot, and this allowed me to do it. The ad in the voice seemed most appealing. So, I called this number, and a woman answered, asking me a few questions about why I considered myself a Don Juan. "How many women had I slept with?" and all those kinds of juicy questions. After I passed the first stage of the interview, I was told to report to this loft. They were going to take some pictures of me in the interview, with my clothes on, also.

I remember a very early Saturday morning when I had to report to this apartment for the interview. I think it was about nine in the morning. I was very hungover, which is quite unusual for me. I don't recall her name; it was probably Pamela or something similar. In any case, I arrived at this photographer's studio, and she started to ask me some questions. She also told me that it was for Forum magazine and that she was pitching the story to them. So, it wasn't sold. Pamela was charming; I think around eighteen.

Pamela asked me a wide range of questions. I think I had been reading too much Brecht at the time. So, I began to elaborate further on what I was saying. I started to talk about sleeping with hundreds of women. Well, I said twelve hundred. Now that's a lie, but anyway, I kept the story going. As you can imagine, I got pretty carried away by the whole thing. I started to go off. When I find women boorish, I leave them. The interview became very heated. She began to ask me about sex and seduction. The most unusual spot of having sex, and if I were a member of the mile high club, "yes, of course." "What is it that I find most attractive in women?" "A great face, good attitude, and hot sex." I went on and on. The interview lasted about an hour. She said that they had interviewed a large number of men. After the interview was over, I thanked her, gave her a warm smile, and shook her hand, then bid her goodbye. I had no idea if this story would ever be printed or what. It seemed uncertain at the time, but it was fun.

That summer in New York was hot, and I was living in a sublet on the Lower East Side, owned by a poet named Damian. I wonder what ever happened to him. The apartment was located on Second Street, between A and B streets. And there were plenty of roaches. The apartment, as I recall, was always messy; newspapers and art everywhere, and that's how they all are.

I was spread out on the futon and quite burnt when the phone rang. It was the middle of the afternoon, and the apartment was unbearably hot. The man on the phone said he was a producer from the Oprah Show and that they had seen the article and were interested in doing a show on Don Juan's. Would I be interested in being on the show? "Are you kidding? Of course I would be." But the article…I had never seen the article and had no idea what it looked like. The producer provided me with a few dates and inquired about my availability. I said that I would most certainly be available on those dates and hung up. My schedule at that time was non-existent.

I ran out to the store to get the issue of "Forum" magazine, but the article was in the July issue, and it was already August. So, I called "Forum" and asked them to send me a few copies. I mean, I was in the magazine, and my vanity did

require a few copies. They became more agreeable after I
threatened to send it to them if they didn't send it to me. I sat
back down on the futon amidst the roaches, newspapers, and
paintings. I was going out with TJ, a beautiful Irish woman, at
the time. Tall, thin, and sweet.

I was very excited to have raised an issue on the Forum. I
thought it was to be my first taste of celebrity. When the package
finally arrived, I could hardly wait to tear into the plain brown
wrapped envelope. I'm surprised that I didn't save the envelope
it came in. I quickly found the article on Don Juan's, and there I
was: a full page with my photo and a small paragraph that had
condensed into my profile. I must admit that the paragraph did
make me sound pretty awful. They had cut out all the sensitive
parts. But there I was wearing a blue shirt with the sleeves rolled
up. My hands were holding my knee in a very canned type of
look, but I wasn't alone. They had selected six other guys to
include in the pictorial. I could hardly contain myself. I called all
my friends and told them. This was big for New York. I thought
it would make me a star, but it didn't; I was just another
exploited individual.

When the producer finally called me back from Oprah, I
gained a better understanding of what was going on. He now had
a firm date. He told me that I would be on the show along with
two other guys, Abn and Teddy. I didn't know them. Don Juan
doesn't usually associate with others. He also told me that there
would be a shrink who had written a book on male sexuality. He
was there, I guess, to figure out why we were so fucked up. I
looked forward to the opportunity. The producer also told me
that I would be staying at the Knickerbocker Hotel in Chicago.
The Knickerbocker had been the old Playboy club. Yeah, that
certainly sounded good to me.

I was flown first class from New York to Chicago. Don't
you love TV? The flight was boring, but the airport turned out

better. Occasionally, in life, there are those serendipitous occasions when things work out. This was to be one of those moments. I was feeling like Don Juan. You can only imagine how dangerous that can be, and it was cause I was loose at the airport. I was walking outside the terminal and taking a bus somewhere. I can't imagine why I was taking a bus, but in any case, I recall walking by this wonderful Italian-looking woman. She was reading a book. Who remembers what it was, but I gave her one of those awful one-liners like... "looks like a good book." She only responded, so I walked ahead and waited a few minutes till the bus arrived.

I like to sit at the rear of the bus. I guess she had a similar idea, and she was a few rows ahead of the last row. I was still interested, so I kept trying to strike up the conversation. "How's the book? Where are you from? Come here often?" I was going nowhere fast, so I decided to play the celebrity angle. I told her I was going to be on Oprah. A breakthrough. "Really?" She said..." on Oprah?" Ahaa, a major discovery. "Yea... well" ...

Oprah and I were tight. "What are you going to be on Oprah for?" Oh, what for? Good question. My brain raced. What was I going to say? Lifestyles. That's right, she's hosting a show on various lifestyles. "Really?" She asked, "That sounds great." Her blue eyes pierced my well... you know. I got turned on. "Listen, I'm staying at the Knickerbocker, Oprah is paying for dinner. Anything we want, the best." Chicks love that. Telling women that you are giving them the best must be an aphrodisiac. In any case, she took down my number, and I got her number, and it seemed like a good match. We chatted a little more, and then we exited the bus. "I'll speak to you later," we agreed.

The Knickerbocker was a great hotel. The room they gave me was beautiful. Two bathrooms in one room. Sheer elegance. Maria called to inform me that she was indeed coming over. Things were looking very. Very good, suddenly.

Half an hour later, the phone rang again. She must be hungry. It was her. She was downstairs. I invited her up to the room. Wow, there was real electricity the moment she entered. She was wearing a skirt. I remember cause, well, it comes into the story later. We talked for a few minutes and then went to the restaurant downstairs. It was very empty. There was just one old guy sitting at a few tables away. We got cozy in our booth.

I ordered the most expensive wine on the menu. I wasn't paying, why not? Everything was the best. I was eating scallops, which are rich in zinc. We got even cozier, and I started to run my hands along her body. It was one of those wonderful moments when everything was working beautifully. We all need a few of those in life. The meal ended, and the dessert was next; I knew exactly what I wanted.

We went back upstairs to my room. Drunk, fed and horny, it only took a few minutes before we were making out. I wanted to go down on her. Why? I don't know, it just seemed like the right thing to do. I was about to start, when and this is the only time, this has ever happened in my life, she lifted her skirt, took off her panties and said to me "I want you to fuck me." Damn, that scared the crap out of me for a moment. After I regained consciousness, I jumped on board. And for the next two hours, we had great sex.

However, it was getting late, and I had to be up at six in the morning. But how could I get rid of her? So instead, we went for a walk. You know, drunk and smelling like sex, cozy in that warm, moist air. Sounds good? Sounds like heaven to me. I wish I were there again. We went back to the hotel, and Maria gave me the book that I had been asking her about. Farewell. What else was there to say? I had her number. Perhaps we would get together again; it didn't matter. Nothing could have been better. I looked at myself in the mirror and I realized that I had been wearing my lucky black shirt. It was almost 2:00 a.m. I had to get up in three hours to be interviewed by Oprah. How cosmopolitan. I was burnt out.

I, of course, felt like shit in the morning. Hung over, exhausted, and wearing a T-shirt. I met the two other Dons in the lobby. Teddy was tall and had dark, curly black hair, and one of those smiles. He told me that he had slept with the girl who was doing the interviews for the Forum. Teddy drove a limousine in his spare time. Ban was a petite, thin musician who made himself out to be a very famous and wealthy person. He told us some stories about being a hit musician. We took a cab together and got to the studio a little late. But we were the stars, except for Oprah, so who cares?

We went to the hair and makeup room to get primed; I mean, we were representing Don Juan. We were all telling seduction stories to each other. So, what happened was that Abn said that he had slept with eight hundred women, Teddy said that he had slept with a thousand, so I told twelve hundred. There was this older guy who was working in the back room, and he had overheard me say that I slept with twelve hundred women—quite an exaggeration. "Twelve hundred… shit, twelve hundred" … he kept saying it over and over again. "Damn twelve hundred women," I can hear him say it.

By the time we arrived at the studio, I was exhausted. But who cares? I had had a sex play all night. I even gave the number to one of the producers in case she wanted to call Maria for a report on how I was. Dangerous, aren't I? I had envisioned they would call her, and she would go on the air and talk about what an incredible lover I was. She refused, and that was that.

I brought a copy of Molière's Don Juan with me to the show. Oprah was her usual warm self and started to ask us about our sex lives and ourselves. But it was Oprah, so it didn't get that graphic. She wanted to know how many women we had slept with, where we met women, and how we met them.

I bragged about my good luck the night before. I could tell she got a little uncomfortable when I started to describe the scene from last night at the hotel she had provided. Whatever. One amusing moment was when Oprah began discussing diseases. Now, AIDS wasn't that bad back then, but it was around. So, I said, "Well, before I have sex with women, I usually check it out, and if it smells funky, then I don't do it." Everyone in the audience made an ick " sound, and we moved on. I did get to read a quote from Moliere, but unfortunately, it didn't translate well on TV.

The show ended, and the three Don Juans were back on their way home—nothing like being a celebrity. As we walked through the airport, women started to cheer us. On the plane, we were celebrities too, and the flight attendants were equally as touchy; I love that.

I got back to New York and remembered that I had a girlfriend at the time. I didn't go into details about the trip; in fact, I don't think I even told her that I was going to be on the show. We had been dating for only a few months anyway. But it didn't help the relationship. Then time went on, and slowly the excitement ended; there was no movie deal, no significant discovery. Teddy took the tape, so I can't even replay it.

But that was fifteen years ago, and now I'm an ageing Don Juan. The story goes that Don Juan is consumed by hell. Is that how I feel? Sometimes. But I guess it's great that I was on Oprah; I mean, how bizarre is that? Makes for a great story. That's it, and well, at least I got laid in Chicago, the windy city.

Chapter 10 Urth Cafe

Back to present tense or past tense in the present. There is nothing as good as the first hour of "Braveheart." I'm sorry, it's so packed with that "let's get them" attitude that I can watch it repeatedly, which I do whenever it's on. It is the kind of story that allows revenge and passion to be expressed. It also features numerous one-liners, as well as blood and gore. It is one of my top ten favorite films of all time.

It's morning, and I'm sitting at the Urth Café. This is a great place to sit, eat, and watch all the beautiful people walk by, as well as the less attractive ones. I have a nasty hangover. It was one of those nights that I sat around watching the Lakers game, talking to friends on the phone. I then got so depressed sitting alone that I had to get out of the house. Los Angeles is a real flake city. There aren't many places where a person can slack off and feel good about it, but Los Angeles is one of them.

So, after all my friends had flaked on me, it was around eleven. I decided to go to my home away from home, the strip club. I needed to see and be with something soft and distant. I just wanted to talk. So, I got into my car and drove over to the Club. The Club, as I call it, was quiet for a Friday night, and as usual, the welcome was warm. I was quickly whisked over to table number 2, where the action was already taking place. I noticed all the usual T and A, and smiled as I saw Cheyenne.

She was wearing a black negligee. Very sexy and see-through. She was also sitting between two guys who appeared to be very happy at their proximity to such a lush piece of ass. I got to talk with Cheyenne later, as she convinced me to move away from the table to the side to speak with her. She had good news,

she said. "Really, what?" "I'm getting married."
"Congratulations," I said, as I stared at her black teddy and
beyond. "When?" "July 5 in North Carolina." "That's great."
She went on to describe her Wedding and all the other details. I
had to think to myself. Is she going to continue stripping?
Whatever. I don't even have a girlfriend, and she's getting
married. That pretty much killed the rest of the evening.

Urth café continued to fill up. Beautiful girls could be
seen drinking coffee and working in the crowd. Sometimes, you
know, I love LA. The Doc just walked in with his nineteen-year-
old girlfriend. That was always quite an enjoyable occasion. His
girlfriend was sitting across from me now. I don't think she
recognized me. Her thin young body was oozing from her
midriff. The doc was doing the ordering. He appeared to have
lost some weight. Must be all that sex. He looked happy, and why
not? A fifty-five-year-old surgeon getting it on with a friendly
and warm nineteen-year-old, sheer bliss. We talked for a
moment after he sat down. He was going to Hawaii for a short
trip. That was what I needed: a vacation. Anyway, he asked me
how things were going, how school was, and if I had a
girlfriend—just the usual. We talked about getting together. I'll
have to call him.

So, guess what happened tonight? That's right, Abby and
I got together. It was one of those things that happen which leave
you feeling fucked up. I guess it was my fault in some ways. I had
called her earlier, but who knew what to expect, except that she
had done a workshop on men and sex. We met at Reds. It was
hard to keep our hands off each other. After about an hour, we
went back to my place, where it didn't take us long to tear off
each other's clothes. The best sex in months. Then it got weird.
Maybe we should have just stayed together. I had plans to get
together with Tess, a good friend of mine. So, Abby and I went
for some cookies at Mani's and then said goodbye. That sucked.

I woke up this morning with the way I felt last night. I was scared to call her. I wanted to call her. But I waited. All I wanted to do was ignore my life. I wanted to get stoned and smoke cigarettes and drink, like Bogey in Casablanca. Of all the Gin Joints in all the cities in all the world, she had to walk into mine.

I had to get out of the city, which was for sure. So, I did what any Californian would do: I got into my car and took off. Malibu was my destination. There is a restaurant there called "Neptune's Net." As the name implies, it's one of those places where you get things from the very mysterious Neptune, namely, Fish. On the Net this morning, it was only a quarter to eleven; I got to select the very Dungeness crab that would be my meal. I felt a little bad about doing it, but I did it anyway. Somehow, I thought it would make me feel better, not killing the crab but eating it. As the day progressed at Neptune's net, motorcyclists would start hanging out there. It was right on PCH, and for you out-of-towners, that's the road that goes along the coast. I had been coming to this place for years. I'm not sure how I found it, but I certainly was glad I did. It was about an hour from where I lived. Now that I was here, I could eat and then slowly make my way back home. I checked to see if Abby had called. She hadn't. What the fuck was I going to do.

I wanted to call Abby and apologize for having seduced her, I mean, I was Don Juan, and she had no chance of resisting. I was going through that "why did I do it phase." As I drove through Malibu, I kept thinking about our future vision together, and that was enough to give me all the regrets I could stand.

When I checked my messages, I had gotten one from my Cuz in New York. Lev was one of those exceptional individuals who had weathered a significant storm and managed to maintain their dignity while creating art simultaneously. She was a few years older than I and was my father's sister's daughter. Aunt Lilly had become a solid ground to help me through all the issues with my mom, and Lev had become my closest contact to family. Lev and her husband had been in an accident with a drunk driver about ten years ago. It was a nightmare. She made it through. Her husband died five years later from AIDS after a blood transfusion. She is a fantastic artist. She has a great loft near Soho that her husband built before he passed away, and Lev filled it with her unique and colorful art. She has two large, long-haired cats with very long names and pedigrees. But Lev is full of heart; her battle with tumors and a missing eye had made her a warrior princess, and I could never spend enough time with her when I was back in New York. She had sent me small pieces of art over the years, a man with a top hat welcoming in the New Year. I had sent her a painting I had done years ago of an angel to watch over her.

Back to Malibu. This time I am at Malibu Colony shopping area, the best of a local, relaxed Malibu hangout. I am at the Coffee Bean, and every three or four seconds, one can overhear someone saying, "totally this," or "totally that." This is a local hangout for families, kids, dogs, and more. There is also a host of overpriced stores featuring all the usual Malibu millionaire items, including candles, jewelry, crystals, and lingerie. Malibu is also filled with beautiful, wealthy women dragging along their husbands. Me, what am I looking for? Everything, since I haven't got anything. There is a steady stream of young women and glamorous model types. This is good for my imagination. Dog owners wander through the plaza, letting strangers have a few minutes with their dogs. It is very white bread here.

Even amid the crowd, I still feel alone. Malibu seems like a family area, and I have no family, not even a girlfriend. I spoke with Abby a few minutes ago. She was fine. I guess having sex didn't affect her like it affected me. That wasn't very pleasant. Now I am thinking about her again. Isn't that annoying? And she is at a fancy restaurant with her parents.

I watch families go by, and I want that too. I give up my thoughts of going to Med school, well, at least for a moment. This day is one more of those nondescript moments in my life where I question what the hell I'm doing.

I went to school. Consider being forty and pursuing a graduate degree. Oh yes, what did I want to be when I grew up? I don't know, and it is driving me crazy. Twice a week, I drove the Beemer through Topanga Canyon Highway; One of the few roads where a wrong turn could send you over a cliff thousands of feet to the ground. It was like driving Le Mans.

At school, I had a class on Group Therapy. This was one of those deep classes that you can get fucked up in. We were working on role-playing, and I placed my mom in a chair and worked on saying goodbye. I told her how much I loved her and how much I appreciated all that she had done for me. I forgave her for the things she did wrong. But mostly I just told her how much I cared about her. However, it was cumbersome, and not a dry eye was in the room. Use this time to get complete, cause none of us live forever.

It was another one of those days that I felt like quitting every other minute. At 9:13, I hated my job; then at 10, I liked my job; then at 11, I wanted to leave. But I stayed, especially since I realized I had only $ 88 in my bank account. That's fucked, I'm sorry, that is fucked. But at least it was eighty, not sixty-six. In any case, I remained at the job. There were some funny moments, like when I started receiving emails in response to the spam I had sent the other day.

TURNING FORTY

There is nothing like the Internet to send out 1,200 letters to different people in an instant without any real overhead. It was my delight, one of the few amusing things that happened to me. I got nasty responses. "Take my name off your Spam list," or "go to hell and take my name off the list," or "I will give you one chance to take my name off the list or else." Or better yet, this one Internet Company accidentally sent me an email stating that they were going to charge me $100 an hour for having to read my letter. Fuck them all. My fantasy was to spam the entire country with a smiley face and a
"Hey, what's up?"

I then signed up for a newsletter email, and before long, I was receiving emails every ten seconds. I signed up for a chat group called Web Justice.

After work, I had therapy, or "the shrink." It was a welcome occasion. I informed my boss that I needed to leave early for a doctor's appointment. I suppose the only kinds of doctors you see after five are psychiatrists. I mean, really, who goes for a checkup after five? In any case, he made some joke about going to see a shrink since I lived in California. I answered that if I lived in Wisconsin, I probably wouldn't need to go to a therapist, I would go cow tipping. My apologies to all the therapists in Wisconsin, and I promise to visit to see exactly what it looks like.

The session was boring; my anxiety was focused on all the other stuff I had to deal with in my life instead of just on my relationship with Abby. Just like the other shrink said, if you kill GOD, then what have you got, whatever that means? My session was about my inability to make any decisions in my life, and how not making any decisions can avoid pain. I talked about how nearly impossible it was for me to throw anything out of my apartment. How hard it is for me to quit my job. Each time I had to make a decision, it wasn't easy. Not all decisions. I could order food OK, but I guess that's different. In the end, it was suggested that I take smaller steps, and that should help. We'll see.

Chapter 11 Snarkali

I'm at the Newsroom café right across from the Ivy. It is one of those Westside types of places where all sorts of famous and not-so-famous Hollywood players come to eat. The Newsroom is where the people who can't afford to eat at the Ivy go: the poor upper-middle class. There are many attractive people here, and I must admit that the two girls who got up from sitting next to me were rather cute. But I was sitting at the bar, which makes it harder to pick up women, but easier to pick up servers.

It might seem like I go from one restaurant to another, but I do work in between. Currently, I am sitting at Snarkali, a restaurant on Melrose Avenue in India. I have a meeting with a friend later tonight to help me with some of my mom's estate stuff. I need something spicy to eat. I can hear the Indians screaming in the background; I wonder what that's about. I used to come here frequently, but I don't come here often at all now. It's like one of those homey, style places that have an Indian feel. Have you ever noticed that Indian restaurants have figured out how to charge for bread? They call it Nan. Would you like some Nan? What kind? Somehow, I managed to order two types of Nan, and when they brought out the second one, I said," I have already had one." "But you ordered this," he said. Scammers, that's it. No more Nan for me. Nan today.

I love LA. I don't care what anyone says, there are so many beautiful women everywhere. I'm back at Mani's. Not that I am going to get any, but at least it's hopeful. Sitting right across from me is this adorable blonde: Short blonde hair, big eyes, sexy body, full lips (the lips I can see that is). She is beautiful. Of course, an actress. What else? She is smoking cigarettes. Well, whatever, she is still beautiful. Across from her is a friend. She is wearing a red hat and blue glasses. I guess she's trying to pick up the scraps. Bet she gets plenty.

I attended the e-commerce show today at the Loews hotel in Santa Monica. Usually, I would feel entirely like a loser, but there was this wonderful marketing expert. We chatted, and I gave her my card. Maybe I'll be lucky, and she'll call. Miracles do happen.

The highlight of the day was when Cynthia, a woman I work with, told me she was going to set me up with a friend of hers. Of course, her name is Abby. Aren't there any other names? Am I getting too old to be set up? That's an excellent question, but who knows? We talked on the phone for about ten minutes. That's a good sign, but I guess I'll have to wait to find out. I have never had a successful blind date. She is a horse trainer. I figured we could go for a ride. She was pretty and sexy. She rode Polo ponies. Blind dates are so fuckin' hard, who knows what to expect? But I was open, and I think so was she. I arrived at her apartment right on time. I mean down to the exact minute, I know it's a bit anal but that's how I am. She was only a few miles from the office. Cynthia told me she was thirty-three, but she looked older. You know the first few minutes were awkward, but then we started talking, and things got better. I didn't know what to do. It's only been a week since I broke up with the other Abby.

How confusing. In any case, she was wearing a hot pink top with plenty of enticing cleavage. At one point in the car, I got a hard-on. How great is that? I was thinking of nailing her, and it happened. I love that. That is the barometer. After all, that's where all my important decisions come from. We chit-chatted at the restaurant. I could tell it wasn't a great mix. But we kept trying. A kind of quiet desperation. But it was friendly.

She recounted an adventure of riding a horse in the ocean. Wow, now that sounded great. She described touching his soft stomach and hearing him make a mooing sound like a cow from delight. Pretty good lunch date, huh? I drove her back to the apartment after lunch. Too bad we didn't have anything to drink. We probably would have been having sex in the car. In any case, I drove her back, and when we got there, I thought that perhaps we could, you know, go up to her apartment. But that didn't happen. She told me that it was too messy. She said she was living with Cynthia, and I guess it was all Cynthia's stuff; in any case, it ended right there.

You know, this reminds me of another time when I did get this girl to let me into her apartment, but she wouldn't let me see her bedroom, so at some point I had to go to the bathroom, and walking by the door, I couldn't help myself. I opened the door to her bedroom, and she was right, it was a mess. It looked like something had exploded. There were clothes on every inch, and underwear everywhere. It scared the hell out of me so much that after shutting the door quietly to the bedroom and having sex with her, I left

Chapter 12 Malibu

Back at Kings Road. Sunday morning. Hung over. Feel like shit. The guy behind me is spouting off about being a financial adviser. I used to be rich. I had saved quite a bit of money, but then I took five months off and blew it. It was a good five months; I wrote three screenplays. But that was history. I sucked down a few coffees at Kings Road, a place where coffee is explosive and then took off.

Today is Mother's Day, and Malibu Lagoon shopping area is filled with the usual assortment of sexy, rich women and fat, pasty tourists. I called my mom this morning to wish her a happy Mother's Day. She was expecting my call, I guess. In her world, she had just had an "invitation only" lunch at some restaurant. I also sent her some flowers. We talked for a few minutes, I told her I loved her, and I was off to Malibu.

No matter what happens elsewhere, the rich are always having kids, and Malibu was filled with them. I don't know, perhaps I was hoping for some beautiful, divorced, wealthy woman with a kid to join me. I was sitting across from a gorgeous blonde with a young child in a swing. She was pushing the child with one hand and talking on the cell with the other. This is Malibu. She leaned over to give her daughter a push, and she revealed some very awesome cleavage. I was in love. She took the time to put a little green sweater on her daughter. Paradise for parents; kids in swings are happy. Next to her was a Japanese couple. The father was in front of the kid, the mother in the back. Next to them was another classic Malibu couple; the bald father leaned on the swing as the child went back and forth. Next to them was a father holding his twins, one in each arm. They were dressed identically in blue hats, pink shirts, and blue and white shorts. Behind me is a Malibu couple arguing; it was brief, and he walked away mumbling. Don't give that marriage long.

Malibu is filled with exotic blondes wearing bizarre clothes. One just strolled by me wearing a T-shirt with a double zero on her chest with the word "juicy" in bright pink letters. Lots of subtext there. I should go after her, but it's so comfortable just sitting here. I imagine that this little Malibu country mart playground is very different from a similar setting in an urban center.

The slide was very popular. A line of five kids waited as other children were climbing all over it.

The father with the twins had put the two of them into one swing and had his other child in the swing next to them. Three at once on the swing, he was well-trained. The two twins were sitting back-to-back in the swing, looking very amazed at the world around them. The dad was enjoying the whole thing. The twins looked very happy. The one that I could see was chewing on her pink shirt. If only I had kids, if only I had a wife, if only I had a girlfriend. The husband showed up to claim the woman with the cleavage. Oh well, I guess it's time to move on. They looked like a happy couple. He put his daughter on his shoulders, and they exited stage right. Children playing are always a source of encouragement: a source of happiness in the world.

One mom wanted her daughter to come and eat. Her daughter didn't want to eat; she just wanted to keep playing. That's the answer to losing weight: keep playing.

Monday, and I'm sunburned. Abby called me while I was in class; she had wanted to come over after class. Fuck. I didn't know what to do. I wanted her to come over, but I started to talk to her about class. In class, we talked about saying goodbye, and before I knew it, we were arguing. Well, I wasn't going to have sex with her tonight. Just as the conversation was getting heated, I cut a little Honda off. So, there I was arguing with Abby driving down Robertson. What a nightmare. I kept asking her how she felt about my asking her how she felt when I talked about saying goodbye. Then she kept asking me why I was asking her. Then, the driver I had cut off pulled in close and tried to cut me off. He kept giving me the finger. I ignored him and continued to talk on the phone. Don't you love LA? Abby and I kept going back and forth with each other. It sucked. I tried to explain the concept of saying goodbye. What was I supposed to do? Get back together with her? She didn't want that, or did she? Whatever, I'm going to sleep. I'll figure it out tomorrow.

Starbucks, at the corner of Crescent and Robertson, sounds like a report from the field. I called Abby from work today, that is, the horse trainer. We could get together for lunch on Friday. It's a new plan. I figure I'm already in that part of town, so why not? Perhaps a little lunch action wouldn't be that bad.

Starbucks isn't that bad, just the usual assortment of investors discussing the market, couples shaking their heads in unison, bald accountants, and yours truly.

I spent the day on the Internet trying to scrape more emails from websites. This is my new challenge: to bring in business. I have sent out over 2500 emails. Boring. Must quit job, mental note.

What was the last test you took? Reflecting on my teaching aspirations, I passed the CBEST test, so I suppose I'm not as unintelligent as I thought. Either that, or the test is so easy. One of my plans is to quit my job and become a substitute teacher. I called to ask what I had to do next, and they asked me what I wanted to teach. I was not sure what to say.

Abby called me ten minutes ago as I was driving. What the fuck am I going to do? Girls on my mind. I resisted the temptation to ask her over. I figure, why start? It's going to be hard to resist. She is singing this Saturday. I am going. When I got out of the car and looked at the phone, I discovered that she had called twice. Last night's rejection made her want me more.

TURNING FORTY

Starbucks always has one cute girl working behind the counter. At least there is something to look at. I am not sure of her name, but she smiled as I ordered my non-fat decaf Grande 150 latte. She seems young. Who else would take the job, I guess? She has one of those kinds of innocent looks; she is a tiger in bed.

I don't usually bet on sleeping with women, but Fred at work just bet me about sleeping with Romano at work. I can hardly wait for her to return. She is a Czech beauty, and she leaves you asking for more. She is at Cannes now, tall and thin, with blue eyes. I must remind myself that it is only Tuesday. I have no chance.

I attended a series of short scenes from my old acting class this evening. I miss acting. All I wanted to do after the show was to quit my job and pursue a career in acting. I hate this day job. The fuckin' Internet. Nothing like sitting in a cubicle all day, staring into space to make you feel like an absolute loser, a tool of society. But I suppose if you're doing something you love, then it's okay. Yeah right. I will hopefully find out someday. And as for the rest of you out there...good luck.

I am sitting with Lamont, discussing my parents' apartment. Bayside is where I grew up; it is not near Harlem. The Guardianship is making me sell their old place, and the government gets to keep the money. It's hard to describe my parents. They were simple people in so many ways.

Lamont came over and talked about his meeting with Mohammed Ali and his inscribed poster. Man, this is worth thousands. Ali wrote ..." It's later than you think." He loved this poster, and we would hear stories over and over about how he met Muhammad Ali and drove with him in his Rolls-Royce. Ali complained that the convertible was too small for him. Lamont would bring his four-piece ensemble over to his house to play.

TURNING FORTY

Lamont was an honored guest. Lamont's walls were covered with photos, Citations, Proclamations, and In Gratitude. There was even a photo of Sinatra; it was that kind of scene. We stayed 'til we were exhausted and then, as usual, I wandered home.

My life was filled with family responsibilities, and there was nothing I could do but try to dive right in. I wish I could take it easy, but the guardianship paperwork was hanging over my head, like the sword of Damocles. It was personal.

I was taking care of all my parents' lack of attention to detail. Paperwork and documents were scattered, and yet my caring for my mother and my thoughts about my dad remained good. I was beginning to have dreams again with my dad. He looked cheery in these dreams, happy and smiling. I would wake up feeling like I had seen him again. Isn't that the amazing thing about dreams?

Yesterday was Saturday, and I knew it would be a long day. I had a double Group therapy class, and it was my turn to be a co-leader. I took the opportunity to do a guided meditation with the group. It was one of my favorites, one of the best ways. I had to leave the planet. It started in the body. Relax your body. Become aware of your breath. Relax your body. Bring awareness to your body. Now bring your awareness to the room. Now bring your awareness to the building. Now it is expanding to the block. Now to Los Angeles. Relax your body. Identify the areas where you still hold tension in your body and release them. Breathe into them. Relax. Now expand your awareness to all of California. Now it is expanding out to North America. Now it is increasing and filling the Planet Earth. Now the solar system. Relax your body. Identify the areas in your body where you are tense and relax them. Let go of the thoughts of the day. Now become aware of the Milky Way Galaxy. Now expand into the group of Galaxies. Now it expands out to the edge of the Universe. Expand yourself. Relax your mind. Identify the areas in your body where you feel tense. Relax. Now I'm starting to come back. We are leaving the edge of the Universe. Bring your awareness back to the Milky Way. Back to the Solar System. Back to Planet Earth and now back to California. Bring your awareness back to Los Angeles. Back to Antioch. Back to the room. Back to your body. Become aware of your body. Relax and slowly open your eyes when you are ready.

OK, we are back in the room. Slowly, people started to come back, and you could see that they were relaxed, and you were too. I loved doing guided meditations, even though sometimes I get nervous and think that I'll screw something up. You must be very focused.

I wish I could say that the rest of the day was relaxing, but unfortunately, that was not the case. I had a baby shower to attend for this girl from school, but I blew it off and went home, then fell asleep for a couple of hours.

I told Abby that I would come to hear her sing at her studio, but the thought of doing that was now disturbing MY peacefulness. She was a good singer, I have to admit. But just the prospect of driving over to Burbank was annoying. I hate driving anywhere. I think this is a family trait. I have heard stories that my grandfather, Gabriel, didn't usually drive.

Abby called me while I was on the freeway to ask where I was and gave me some more directions. As I got closer, I called her to let her know that I was going to grab a bite to eat first, a slightly tense moment. She was not pleased with this, I mean, how could I be hungry at a time like this? Whatever. Freedom? A few minutes later I was sucking down some fish tacos.

The studio where she was singing was a big, empty room. I ran into one of her friends and an acquaintance named David. He was a sculptor, and he told me about living at home with his father and the ease of his life. He had been invited to Hawaii and

Africa to visit friends there. I couldn't help but fantasize about taking a trip anywhere and relaxing. Abby's singing was beautiful, and as usual, I found myself oscillating between loving her and wanting to get out of the room. Isn't that always the case? Good girl, bad girl - a tough decision.

It was Saturday Nite, and I drove home wondering what the fuck I was going to do. When I got home, I had a call from Mucci, a good friend. He mentioned that he was going over to Bar Nor and told me that he would call me later. He never did. So, I decided to go to the strip club so the night wouldn't be a total loss.

The strip club was packed with quite an assortment of characters. Just as I arrived, two guys were moving things in and out of their Bentley. What it was, I don't know, and it's probably well I don't ask. I had a half-price ticket for the club; I had been there too often. Inside, it was tough to find a seat. The girls seemed excited; they were putting on a little extra show. It was as if they were on some drug; a couple of girls were flirting and teasing each other. I found myself turned on and wanting to throw money to make them happy. It was a vicious circle, and it never did seem to end until I left the club... and hit the cold air of L.A. My life did seem hard right now, and the strip club somehow made me forget about everything except one thing: sex.

I found myself amid the most challenging things in my life; summarizing my parents' estate - how does one do that? I am having the hardest time imaginable trying to figure out not only the paperwork but also all the numbers. This isn't one of the things I do well. I should have paid someone to do this for me. It's hot in my apartment, and I'm wired on caffeine, and I'm sure I'll be up all night.

I pulled a rune, and that sometimes helps. "Undertake this passage joyfully," the rune commands. "Struggle means breakthrough." OK, here I go. See how everything makes sense with the runes.

Chapter 13 Day in Vegas

I spent the day in Vegas. I lost at the casinos and won at the airport. What happened was that I wanted to do a little gambling while we were in Vegas, and Fred wanted to go home. You know, I'm a loving wife and have three cute kids, so I said... "Well, how about ten minutes?" Anyway, I lost at roulette. Lost to 00, if you know what I mean. By the time we arrived at the airport, we had just missed a flight by ten minutes. The next flight was three hours away, so we went to the Bar and got drunk. After two thirty-two-ounce beers and a shot of Midori and vodka I was fucked up just in time to get onto the flight.

We got a flight that was an hour earlier. This was Southwest Airlines, so we were given numbers. By the time we got on, there were only a few seats left. Fred sat in the back and looked as though he was going to pass out, so I went to the front. In the front, the seats are facing one another. I sat across from this adorable blonde named Stephanie. There were six people in the group, including one girl who tried to ignore us altogether. She was reading a book on Buddhism while listening to her headphones. Who knows what she was listening to? However, the rest of the group was going to be a lot of fun. Stephanie had a four-year-old named Brandon. On my right was a very dark-haired woman named Cindy, who had three kids. On my left was a man named Sean, who had three kids, and in the far corner was Len, a huge fifty-year-old Greek chef for Marriott. I told them that I had had six beers- I didn't mention the shot. In any case, a lively discussion ensued as I systematically asked each person about their life. It was perfect; the flight was only an hour long, and before I knew it, it was over. The group thanked me for keeping them together. Sean added that usually there are just a bunch of assholes. I suppose we were ahead of that by a long shot.

When I finally got home from Burbank Airport, which is a much easier place to find my car than LAX, I realized how exhausted I was. I slowly moved to the bed and collapsed, and it was only around ten. I was awoken by Diana, "What? I'm sleeping; I'll talk to you tomorrow." At around 12:30, Abby called from Hawaii. She was working hard at a yoga retreat, rough being a millionaire. I was too tired to answer the phone. I tend to be very sappy when I answer in the middle of the night anyway.

Diana gave me this wisdom: Ford…Found on Road Dead, Saab, let's hear some Saab stories. Car stories: Hollywood is filled with them. This just happened: An accident occurred down the block from where I live. I rush out of my apartment. A car and a Ford truck collided at the intersection of La Brea and 6th. I called the police. The couple inside the car is fine. They are from Hong Kong and work for The Walt Disney Company. A thin Latino drives the truck; he looks fine, but the woman is slightly injured, and their car is badly smashed. But they work for Disney. The Fire Department EMT comes over and checks them out. They are confused; they think he is a Fireman, so they don't mention the injury. I went back and got him. When suddenly, he finds out that they work for Disney: "Do you know Carol Simmons?" he asks the guy who was in the accident. He replies, "Sure," and suddenly, they are talking about Disney. Who cares about the accident? I've got a script to sell. The cars are smashed and in pieces, strewn all over the street. The cops don't want to fill out a report. I tell the guy to make sure they fill out a report. The Cop says with one of those, "I could always shoot you," looks. We're taking care of it. Fine. Whatever. I have had enough for one night. Only in L.A. So, if you work for Disney, you might get off if you can listen to a script pitch after a big car accident. I was going to pitch one too... but I resisted— Hell of a night.

Back in LA and over at Lamont's. I have already described him in some detail, but let me continue. Lamont would always get pissed that I would come over to party and not bring any girls with me. Well, I wouldn't for many reasons. Let me illustrate. Have you ever met someone you didn't know, but through a series of accidental meetings, you began to feel comfortable? That happened to me about a year ago. I kept bumping into this woman in my neighborhood. I was single at the time, and she seemed nice, so we started talking. Before I knew it, I was taking down her number and planning a dinner with her.

Ellen was charming, funny, and Jewish—something Jewish guys worry about sometimes. Anyway, we talked on the phone and agreed to get together Saturday night. Great, I thought, but then Mucci called me and announced that he was having a party at his pad in the hills, and I was requested to attend.

Usually, I would never take a first date to a friend's, as it's just too much for a first date. However, it was Mucci, and all my friends were going to be there, so I thought, why not? I picked Ellen up, and we went to a French restaurant that no longer serves Parmesan cheese. You know how the French get sometimes. Anyway, we had a lovely dinner and a bottle of wine—pretty good buzz. I'm thinking, "Maybe I don't want to go to the party," but I give in to my better judgment and go anyway. The ride to Mucci's was a very curvilinear route through Mulholland Drive, and the Beemer took the turns like a pro. I was feeling like Mario Andretti, and so I showed off to the girl. I didn't notice at first, but she was turning green.

In any case, we arrived at Mucci's late. Everyone was already drunk, especially Lamont, who must have consumed an entire bottle of scotch. Now, when he is drunk and pissed, he can be scary. He is short, and I would guess he is close to three hundred pounds. Usually, he was like a sweet bear, but not tonight. I would have liked to avoid the introduction, but there was nothing I could do: he was standing in the doorway. So, I introduced him to Ellen, and he started to give her a big hug, a huge one. It was odd cause she was facing outward. He kept hugging her, then he began to strangle her. She was trying to get loose, and he kept on. I tried to grab his arms to release her, but he was so drunk that he kept laughing.

Ellen, who was already green from my driving, started to turn a little purple. I tried to pull him off, but he wouldn't release her. After a couple of minutes, he let go. Ellen didn't say anything, but I had the feeling that not only was I not going to get any action tonight, but I would probably not get a second date. I was right. She wouldn't return my calls, so I guess that was the end of that.

So, I was at his house when he started to give me a hard time about not bringing anyone over. He would say, "Ann, Robin, Lonnie, you should call them and Scott," the skinny, flute player. She builds wax…things, we should call them. Then he would start on the alcohol. "You got the cheapest scotch." He would give me endless drag, and I would bark back. Tony Bennett was singing in the background. I guess if you don't have it, you don't have it. I would be sitting in Lamont's living room, with the three oversized red chairs with lion heads made in some mysterious place that he wouldn't mention. Those were fun times, and Lamont was a good friend even with the drag and the choke hold on the babe, oh, and by the way, for the next few weeks, I would introduce him as the strangler.

Mickey was a sexy and saucy Russian who worked behind the counter at King's Road. She was a singer, but she wouldn't sing, no matter how much Peter (an old next-door neighbor) and I tried to convince her. It's a little muggy out there. It's smog. Face it, it's smog. This is LA. It's smog. Not fog, but smog. They lined up to get that caffeine-infused coffee. What happened to your film? It's glossy. I don't think everyone gets that movie. Mickey was wearing a giant hat like something out of a Dr. Seuss book.

Inside King's Road was the coffee session. I was getting very weird. Forty and wired, yes, that was my life. Peter left, and we agreed that if either one of us made it, we would buy each other drinks for life. Great, poor, and drunk, a great way to live. Mickey complained about a green card. Winning a green card. Once you apply, it takes four years. Then Rod Stewart's drummer, who was sitting at our table, also joined in. As an American citizen, I always felt slightly removed from the whole experience.

Okay, so I picked Abby up from the airport, and yes, we spent the night together. Why is that? I tried to resist, but it wasn't easy. I picked her up, and we weren't in the car for five minutes when she started to cry. Chicks and crying, what the fuck? She had just returned from Hawaii; why would anyone be crying? I knew then that there was no way that I was going to drop her off. It was going to be dinner and all the accompanying drag. I suppose hearing about her week-long vacation isn't a particularly upbeat story for me. I needed a vacation… no question about that.

We returned to her apartment, went to dinner, and then came back. She still had my toothbrush, although I think she was using it to clean the bathroom. I woke up at 8 am and sneaked out of the apartment. She picked her head up and asked me where I was going. "I 've got work to do," and I exited.

I ended my therapy today. That was hard. I imagined myself all day telling her that I was going to leave, and I had a hard time even saying it to myself. I don't know why, except that I must have been yelled at for quitting something before in my childhood. It's all about childhood. I must say that it went well. I ended it and it was OK.

Abby called me while I was in therapy. Probably while I was talking about her, she not only called me on my cell phone, but also at home. It's funny cause although I want it to end, I know I will miss her a lot and there's nothing I can do. But there is that cute little Irish girl in the short red dress I met this weekend.

It was Saturday, the second-to-last day in my "family systems" class. Everyone brought in a poster. I decided to use Canvas. I started cutting out articles with lots of family diagrams. I was also looking for stories on families. I flashed back to what's left of my family—I spoke to my mom yesterday. In any case, I cut out this article from the Hollywood Reporter regarding a murder that had taken place on Charlie Chaplin's estate in Geneva. Wonder what that place looks like? Anyway, this article described a horrible scene of a husband cutting off his wife's head and then killing himself. I pasted the article on the canvas and surrounded it with red pastel. I then covered the red pastel with a transparent layer, but the clear covering smudged the red pastel all over the piece. By the time I finished the piece, I had used a lot of red, and it began to resemble a big red mess, like a murder scene. When I explained the piece to the class, it seemed like a crime scene. I might have scared the class. I hear them quiet down as I explain the decapitation. I think I scared them all right. They said it was very effective. Guess I won't be getting any dates from that group.

After class, I went to have lunch with Abby. I had tried to get out of it the night before, but no such luck. Oh, wait, a side story. Abby called me Friday night, very late and very drunk. She wanted me to come over. She begged me to come over. I was way too tired, even seriously, to consider it. Abby didn't even remember the call on Saturday. Anyway, I was on my way over to pick her up. I promised myself that I would not sleep with her; at least I would resist the temptation. When I got over to Abby's, she was still in her pajamas, as she would say. We had a moment together, and then before I knew it, I was lying on the couch with her on top of me. She had some very nice new underwear to show me, which was a lovely shade of purple. The phone rang. It was Ruth, the girl whose party we met at. Ruth was getting married in less than a month. We joked on the phone about where we were going to go. I was in the middle of suggesting sushi or Chinese, and before I knew it, we were on our way to meet Ruth.

I was driving my car for a change, so I would have more control when we left. It was always my intention to make it short. Of course, that wasn't going to happen.

Ruth was like any bride-to-be, all excited and talking about her dress and flowers alternately. It seems her grandmother was making her wedding dress by hand, which is very impressive. They have visited a few stores to browse dresses, but you are not allowed to take photos of the wedding dresses on display. It is a highly guarded secret, akin to photographing art at an opening. You were not allowed to take any pictures, fearing that other brides would discover the secret stitch and the secret would get out. All kinds of espionage material are very intriguing to me, I must admit. In any case, Ruth reviewed the whole menu with us. I kept asking questions: What is the appetizer? What is the main course? What kind of cake? All the standards.

The question of where I was sitting arose, a delicate one. I didn't know what to say. It got awkward. Abby got up to go to the bathroom, and I started to get into it with Ruth. Why did you ask me like that? It was mean and she knew it. But what the fuck was I going to say sitting there right next to her? She asked me if we were still going out. "No," I said, "and why did you ask me like that in front of Abby. What the fuck was I going to say?" She paused, and just as she was about to answer me, Abby came back. The two of us were quiet, like we had been plotting. It was a real pregnancy pause. The seconds seemed like years. I then added, "So, how do you feel, Ruth?" and the conversation began again. However, it was time to leave the restaurant, so after the weird moment, we got up. That made everything seem even more bizarre. We got into the car. Abby sat in the front, but the ride had an elephant-in-the-room feeling. After a few minutes, they dropped me off at Abby's. She remained in the car with Ruth to visit the party place and browse items for her wedding.

I was driving when the cell rang. It was Abby. She argued with Ruth and got out of the car, needing a ride. Could I pick her up? So, I just made a U-turn on Olympic and picked her up at the Chevron. We went back to her house, but didn't have sex. I think she was disappointed. In any case, I got out after about an hour, and I was free.

Chapter 14 Sex Therapy

On Thursday, the 8th, I had expected to have a somewhat calm day. Well, not entirely quiet. I was planning a lunch with Abby, not my Abby, but another Abby. I knew it wouldn't work from the start, but I figured I'd give it a try. I was running late, and it was very hot outside. Abby had a rider's frame. Big hands, blonde hair, you know the kind. Who cared about what she was cooking? All I wanted to do was jump her.

It was our third lunch. I think that's the proper amount of time. She asked me if I was planning on being a sex therapist. I, of course, said yes. I said yes as I ran my hands all over her body. Ooh, she liked it, and she was very lively. Our teeth clanged. And we continue to make out. After a while, she suggested that we sit down on the couch. I agreed. So, we started to make out on the couch. After a few more minutes of grinding, I thought I'd check out what was going on underneath. But she stopped me. Fuck. I was so ready. What's up with that? She told me I was overstepping boundaries. I agreed with her. That confused the situation. She smiled. I stopped. I hate that, just when things are going well. But I wasn't that interested in her; she lived too far, deep in the forbidden valley. Remember: location, location, and location, just like real estate.

Time moved on, and I had to return to the office. Well, she threw me out as well. So, I went back to the world of dot com.

The last few days at work had been especially boring and pressured. The $200 million owner was wondering when the bacon would be arriving, so they asked me repeatedly at the e-commerce meeting. I tried to explain what I was doing and who I had called, but frankly, the list was getting shorter. I was so busy doing everything else. And fuck, they offered no real support. I was sick of carrying a company that had no budget without continuously kissing the ass of the owner. What the fuck. I hated this job, but I stuck with it. I think this is based on my high tolerance of pain.

Then I got the email asking me to list out all the shit I had going on. This was for Mr. Big himself sitting in the mansion in Beverly Hills. I suppose he was wondering why he was spending $75,000 a year on me. I was under investigation, it seems. Not really, but I did have to pay the day figuring out the approach to take in listing all my essential conquests of the day. My boss was wondering exactly what I was doing. I assured him that I wasn't writing any book and if I was, it certainly wasn't on his time. "I'm not running a business on the side," I told him. He seemed amused, and he started to grin. Good time to exit, I thought, so I went back to my desk and began to hack out a list. I hate cold calling. It was the worst. At least emails are distant. About a year ago, I got a part in this low-budget recreation of a TV show, called "Missing something, etc." It was very strange that I just happened to be watching TV when it came on. It was June 8th or 9th.

There I was on cable. The story was that this religious group had kidnapped my TV wife and children. In the scene I was watching, I was in combat gear and inside a coffee shop, working out a plan to take over the compound. Well, I was trying to get my wife out.

It was very strange to see myself on TV. It was very odd. It was paranormal. Something was going on that made me watch that show at that time. I don't usually watch the learning channel. I love acting, but after watching this, I need to find some better material and work on losing weight.

At the office, I was on a roll. I had attempted to negotiate a deal with Atom Films for retail distribution. That is the key to the internet and supply-side economics: providing a retail revenue stream as well. However, it's challenging to handle the packaging, marketing, and content. I was amazed to see the deal start to come together. But then it almost left me. On Friday, our contact was supposed to come back. See… I am working on putting deals together.

I spent some time with Lamont last night. We got stoned. He kept trying to sell me some, but I refused. Of course, this morning I had a horrible brain death. My brain wasn't working at all. It took me an hour to find my car, and I was parked in the neighborhood. I went around and around the block. Up one street, down the other, and finally there it was, two cars down from a similar-looking model, the M6, its 350-horsepower cousin. I hate it when I do that. That's why I stopped getting high, I could never find my car or remember my shit. That's fucked up.

So here I am once again at King's Road sucking down an iced latte in the to go section. It's pretty cozy here, just James. Brown in the background, with the smell of coffee all around me. Patrons walking in and out order all sorts of coffee concoctions, though they are usually much more normal than at Bean or Starbucks.

I was in dating mode again and boy did it suck. It was going to be a very lonely Saturday night unless I could come up with a plan. My massage therapist, who comes to the office, was planning to dance tonight. I thought that could be the thing to do…but it was in Glendale. The horse trainer had offered to take me to a party, but I could see that I wasn't really in the mood to be on her date. There was something about her living in the valley that bothered me.

I had a sort of date with a girl from school the other night. It was more of an odd evening than a date. We went to

Farfalle. A local Italian restaurant where the servers often try to take advantage of you on a date. In this case, I knew she wasn't that easy, so I figured her Teflon exterior would take care of any of the servers, and I was right. Dating is so hard. All I want to do is have sex the first time I meet any potential, and if I don't want sex, then it's not happening. That is the test. With her, I found her cute, another word that is the kiss of death. I wanted to make a pass, but I could see that it was going to be a tough call.

At the end of the evening, after I paid the fifty-dollar bill, we had an awkward hug. Then I walked her to the car, and she gave me a lift back to my car. We then kissed on the side. That is, I kissed her on the side of her face—end of story.

I am typing this on a flight to New York. It was one of those business trips I look forward to. Abby drove me to the airport. I figured, why not? I drove her to the airport last time. Besides my business trip, I also took the time to start cleaning up my parents' apartment. This project might be compared to picking up sand on the beach. I knew it was going to be a tough trip, and I could feel the difficulty in getting it started.

The flight was made slightly better by having this beautiful Swedish woman sitting behind me. She worked for a photographer and was also studying photography at SMC. "I was thinking about studying there," I told her. "Oh really. What would you be studying?" "I was thinking of studying piano," I said. I know how to play the black keys, but I wanted to learn the white ones. Anna was her name. Blue eyes and blonde hair. Mental note: must take vacation in Sweden, no matter what.

Earlier today, Boston University, my alma mater, as they say, mailed me an alumni directory from 2000. I immediately looked up my name to see if I was listed and what it said, and there I was. I was listed as having worked at Bacons, a former employer. I was wondering about all my ex-girlfriends. They should have had a few other indexes besides just alphabetical and by school. They should have had one by first names or by nicknames. I was trying to figure out the last names of all these ex-girlfriends. I'm sure a lot of them have new names. I mean, whatever happened to Olivia or Sharon? I hated that. I wanted to take the book with me on the flight, but I realized it was too heavy, so I left it behind.

New York should be fun, even though I have to do all this cleaning. The funny thing is that I'm not very good at cleaning. Just imagine how I might be at cleaning their place. I hadn't called any of my old cronies; I just figured that when I got there, I would decide who to call, if anyone. I shared with Fred that I once had a lovely girlfriend in NY. Her name was Emi. We had this brief affair. I remember her so well. She had big blue eyes and huge breasts. She thought that we might make a good match, so she flew out to LA to see if I wanted to get married to her. Marriage? I had never thought about that. She arrived using a cane. A little too much victim energy for me, I thought, but I went along with it. After a few days, the two of us, on my small single bed, were experiencing growing pains. She was too many women and we started to argue. She was the only girlfriend that wanted to give me a blowjob with a condom on. A condom for a BJ? I knew we were in trouble, but I went along with the game. In the end, it was her driving that I couldn't stand. She spent the rest of her time with her girlfriends. Several months later, when I was in New York and wanted to take action, I called her, and she answered the phone. She said, "I'm married," and hung up on me, and that was it.

I joked with Anna, the girl from the flight, about Sweden. The Swedes are very attractive but not particularly funny. She didn't laugh at my piano joke, and I don't know why. She did mention that she liked yoga and was doing it over at Brian's class in Santa Monica. Now there's a reason to start doing yoga again. I should have been a yoga teacher. What could be better? I thought. Anna was now quietly watching the movie. Well, I guess that's it for our conversation. She told me that she had painted her Volvo and her apartment the same color. I was very intrigued, to say the least. I gave her my business card and said goodbye.

I just got back from the Paramount hotel, a spot where one can drink good red wine and watch the pandemonium of New York at the same time.

My next adventure in NY was much more of a family thing. I had given myself the task of cleaning my parents' apartment, which was no small task at all. Did you ever imagine that a job like this would be necessary? I didn't. I am certainly not prepared. My parents were antique dealers. Did I mention that before? They collected more stuff than could be believed, wall to wall junk. Brick and brac is another name for shit, everywhere. And as my mom got more insane, she bought even weirder stuff like thousands of hair barrettes.

So, I walked into the apartment, looked around, and immediately went out to get a double latte. This was going to take reinforcements. I came back and sat down on one of the antique rockers, smoked a clove cigarette, which I hardly ever do, and looked around.

I imagined my days as a kid, flashbacks. I could see my old bedroom and the way the apartment once looked years ago. It was that time. I walked around the place. It was such a mess that it was hard to look at. There were boxes stacked everywhere, as well as clothing. I tried to donate the clothing and even some of the furniture, but no one wanted it, no one. Can you imagine that feeling? I wanted to give away good junk, and nobody wanted it. I suppose I'll have to drop it all off. I spent the day discarding various papers and documents. It's funny how, after a while, things that were so important mean so little.

After all that cleaning, I was definitely in the mood for something fun. It just so happened that Kyra, Mucci's girlfriend's twin sister, was in New York visiting her new boyfriend, so I decided to see them. We met outside his apartment. They didn't even invite me in. How odd. What were they hiding? We met and walked over to the Hudson River to look. It looked wonderful at sunset. We then went to a very spicy Thai restaurant for dinner. After dinner, we went to one of their friends' apartments for a party.

It was a very unusual party for me to attend, as it was a Wedding celebration. We all raised our glasses to toast the happy couple with champagne. They were Europeans, so the champagne was good, and after about thirty minutes, Kyra and the new boyfriend wanted to leave to go to a strip club called VIP. Did someone mention strip club?

Now I don't need to mention that I'm OK with strip clubs, but the idea of going with a woman always seemed odd to me. But whatever, I figured it would be fun. However, I did realize that I needed to return reasonably early since I was staying with my aunt, Lilly, in Great Neck. Yes, I know, I was slumming. In any case, I agreed to go to the club. We paid the twenty-dollar cover, and we were in.

The show was on a center stage with women on the floor giving out lap dances. The floor was filled with soft, comfy chairs with wheels. There were most certainly a lot of T and A. I got a chair close to the stage and watched the show go on. Nothing special at first, until Cindy.

Cindy was one of those rare beauties who left me speechless. I couldn't take my eyes off her. She was wearing a two-piece red dress with dark red lips. She had long curly black hair with very slender legs. We connected. She stared at me, like I stared at her. Well, not the same. She danced and danced for quite some time. I was in awe. My friends could see that she was looking at me. After she was done, she walked right over to me and sat on the side of the chair, and we talked for a while

I learned a great deal about Cindy. She was from Brooklyn and wanted to be an actress. When she talked, I could hear a cute accent like a lisp. She had a manager that she complained about, and she didn't like her headshots. I told her she was wonderful and that she should take back her power from the manager. I did my best to help as much as I could. Then my friends interrupted this beautiful moment we were having by offering to get me a lap dance. Shit, the moment was so real. It broke the tenderness. But the lap dance was perfect. She brushed her hair against the side of my face. I told her how great she smelled. She told me that she had been on Howard Stern as a virgin. I asked her if she was. She laughed. I told her that I had been on the Oprah show.

I don't think she knew who Oprah was. She hasn't done any films yet. I suggested student films, but her manager disagreed. Please get rid of him... I'll help you. She then rubbed and gyrated herself all over me. It was heaven except that it was going to end. I asked her if she would go out with me. She said she was going out of town. I gave her my number and told her to call me. I didn't even have a card, so I wrote it on one of those pink coffee bean cards. I was sad to have to go.

I drove home dreaming about Cindy. I imagined her calling me and my sending her a first-class ticket to LA. Of course, I picked her up in my Porsche or Aston Martin; I tried both versions. She was pleased to see me, and then we drove to my house in Malibu. I tried several different houses in my mind. We had sex as soon as we got home. I tried several different positions in my mind. It was amazing. Then I alternated between getting her a Hollywood job and marrying her. In any case, it was great.

I could hear her Brooklyn accent in my head as I sped down the Long Island Expressway in my rent-a-wreck vehicle. It didn't matter. I kept thinking of her over and over. The pain of falling in love. I hated that. I looked at the cell phone. It was 1:22 am, shit. I should have just stayed at the club, but I wanted to get home reasonably early.

When I finally arrived at Lilly's, it was almost one-thirty. That sucked, but what was I going to do? I stood outside the door and called her on the cell. She said, "Where the hell are you?" "I'm downstairs." "Oh? Ok, I'll be right down."

I waited, and after a few minutes, I could hear her come down the steps. Then I heard a loud thump, and she started to scream. "Oh no," she said I'm bleeding. Shit I was locked out. Everything raced through my mind: I've killed my aunt, I killed my aunt, oh my god, what have I done. I've done this. Please, I'll never go to another strip club again, never do it again, promise, swear to God.

No, she was OK. She was talking. She opened the door. Her head was bleeding. There was a two-inch cut in the back of her head. I helped her into the kitchen and then, in that state of panic, and of course still having the remnants of a buzz, I called 911. Then I called the Great Neck police, and then I called her son. I didn't know what to say or do. "It's all my fault," I kept thinking. I waited anxiously for the police to arrive. It was one forty-five am.

When the police came, I felt guilty. Yes, officer, it was I, I did it. Please don't shoot me. I confess. There were two squad cars. The lights were flashing. It was a scene against the magnificence of the oaks that lined the street. I was freaking out inside and the night was going to be long. We were on our way to the hospital, and it was two in the morning. The memories of the Paradise strip club were far removed from the ER. They put her into an ambulance, which I followed closely. They told me not to go through any lights, but I figured fuck it, what are they going to do-give me a ticket?

The emergency room was filled with the usual victims. I noticed two cute doctors. But they were both married. One must have been Indian. She had a beautiful smile, big eyes, and even some cleavage. I flashed back to Cindy. It all seemed so far away.

Lilly had the usual X-rays and a CT scan. I stood next to the guy doing the scan. Slowly, the inside of her entire head appeared on screen in multicolored, three-dimensional detail. I kept thinking that the insides of my head might look similar, since we were related. The doctors kept referring to her head as a coconut. "Quite a coconut you've got there," and "let's see inside that coconut."

They decided to use staples instead of stitches. Lilly and I joked about them taking a stapler to her head. She laughed, and I felt a little relieved. I apologize for coming in so late. I didn't want to apologize too many times, lest she think I had done it, and no, I never mentioned the strip club. Are you crazy? The Indian doctor came over; she was more beautiful up close.

By the time we left, it was 5:00 a.m. Lilly directed me home. Nice Nite. Cindy seemed like a long time ago. Lilly was such a trooper, I can't even say enough. I love her. If it were the other way around, I'd probably be quite hysterical. Are you kidding? A two-inch gash on the back of my head? I'd be ballistic. In any case, we wobbled back home in my rent-a-wreck. My millionaire Aunt Lilly and I. It was so late when we finally walked through the door that we exchanged a few words. She carefully walked up the long staircase lined with a million dollars' worth of art. I walked behind, slowly, not knowing what to say or do, how to apologize. We agreed that she would lend me the spare key.

I woke up the next morning around ten or eleven, to the sounds of aphids chirping in the background. It was beautiful and warm outside. I opened the little balcony door and took a deep breath. The Oaks had a much friendlier look in the day: its beautiful front lawn and, across the street, a vast, lovely house with white brick and a Volvo in the driveway. Kids walked up and down the street. Families went for walks—the sounds of birds and the soft tapping of the opulence of society. Then suddenly, the night flashed back in my mind. I wondered how Lilly was doing. I opened the door and went downstairs, turned on the TV, and waited for her to get up. She shuffled down about thirty minutes later. The bandage was quite visible, and she looked pretty good considering what the nephew had caused. I told her I was going to clean out my parents' house. She wished me luck, and I was on my way.

Chapter 15 Dimension of time

Cleaning out my parents' house is undoubtedly one of the most challenging things in my life that I've ever had to do, or, I would add, that anyone anywhere in the universe would ever have to do.

I am inside the three-bedroom apartment, and everywhere I turn, there is something from my past. Since my parents were antique dealers, there were endless boxes of assorted items. The dimension of time is bent; it is a time warp. All the layers are overlapping. Next to some old hospital bill is a card congratulating my parents on my birth. Next to that is a note from me from camp when I was ten, giving them a list of foods to bring on visiting day. Dry-roasted peanuts are at the top of the list.

I come across endless phone books from my dad. I found a giant birthday card from his sixtieth birthday in 1983. I saw my note on the card. I pause to look at the card and flash back to the memory of the dinner.

Scissors are everywhere, old ones, new ones, big ones, and small ones. My back is killing me. Lots of photos of all the relatives and friends. I find an envelope marked "personal." Inside is a note written in red saying, "I, Joey ...borrowed 7500 as a personal loan from Sol." What exactly was going on back then? The note is dated 7/18/84. I toss it.

Bills, bills, and more bills, and most of them never even opened. I certainly won't open them. There was everything expected, including his death certificate. I don't know how you can look at your father's death certificate without taking a deep breath and a tear, and that was what I did. A long pause, a tear; the whole scene was overwhelming.

While I was going through all this, they were installing a new Cardinal in NY, so there was very melodic music playing from the TV in the background. It made everything more dramatic, as if that was needed.

Then I came across stacks of old photos, most of which were from the wartime years. My dad was in his twenties and looked like he was having a grand old time. There were family photos and shots of him with his cronies in Acapulco. He seemed very happy.

I must have filled up twenty bags of assorted trash and fifteen bags with old clothes. I found a place that would take all this great stuff. I also included a few hundred hair barrettes that my mother had purchased last year as a new addition to our selection.

I went through all of my mom's clothing; I didn't put any on. I remembered her wearing them: the one she wore to my Bar Mitzvah, and everything was familiar, all the clothes she had been saving. All those silk dresses and exotic accessories she would never wear again—if she had ever worn any of them. Then, in the closet next to the bathroom, I found a plastic bag containing old samples from hotels and similar establishments. I was pretty surprised when I saw two small containers of shampoo from Ruby Foos, a hotel our family had stayed in about thirty years ago. I remember Ruby Foos very well: it was an exotic French Chinese place, and we had some lobster with fried rice. They served us just one plate each. It was extraordinary. I tossed the miniature shampoos in my car and headed to the thrift store to get rid of them all.

My poverty was affecting me. I thought about Lilly talking about everyone buying houses. I could feel myself starting to cry inside. All this stuff is in my parents' house. And still, I'm poor. It's time to head to the thrift store to donate more items. If only they had collected diamonds or gold coins, everything would be easier. I did find this diamond bracelet. At least I thought it was until I brought it to the jewelry store. The guy didn't even have to hold it to know it was fake. Too bad, I thought that would have been very nice and very surprising.

So, I brought 10 bags of my mom's favorite clothes to the thrift store and donated them. I also threw in the mink stole. What am I going to do with it? Make it into a piece of art? Well, yes, but anyway. Inside the thrift store, there are two older women and two older men. They asked what I had brought in, and when I told the man about the mink stole, he wondered which bag it was in.

TURNING FORTY

My body is killing me. I received a massage last night before going out, and I think she felt responsible for correcting all the irregularities in my skeletal system; as a result, I'm experiencing pain today when moving.

I'm sitting at Starbucks at Northern Blvd and 215th Street. Sting plays in the background. The air conditioning is freezing my back. Pier 25a is across the street. We had my father's birthday there. It seems like a long time ago. I miss him. If only I had insisted that he stay with me in California. I should have moved the whole family. They never moved from that apartment. Forty-five years in one place. It nearly killed me when they turned off the phone. I called the number, and some guy answered. Forty-five years with the same number. That hurt. No phone there now. No reason for it. It is quiet.

I got back to Lilly's. My back is killing me, I'm so tired, and I smell. All I can do is lie down. Lilly walks up to me and asks if I want to rest a little or if I'm in a rush to get something to eat. I can barely move, so I ask her, "Do I look like I'm in a rush?" She laughs and exits. One thing about my aunt is that she often sleeps with the TV on. It's blasting so loud that I can barely believe anyone can sleep, but she does. Of course, I can hear every word. It's hard to rest, but I collapse into bed.

We decided to visit a local Italian restaurant. I asked her if we could take the Benz, my rent-a-wreck is making weird sounds. So, I feel like a chauffeur behind the wheel of the 500 SEL. As I drive, I try to line the road up with the chrome emblem on the hood. At dinner, Lilly tells me the story of her Gefilter fish, and a great poet named Crossover from England, who tried her fish only to look all over England for it. Hmm, Gefilter fish. Nice thought, but I must try to sleep. I think I'll try the floor. My back is killing me.

TURNING FORTY

I lay on the floor till the early part of the morning. I was hoping for a complete recovery, but no such luck. My body aches and hurts in most positions. So, I go back to bed and quickly fall asleep. Lilly's morning routine awakens me. I wait in bed thinking that each minute will help my back.

Lilly had this habit of banging on the door and then pushing it open. However, the door to the bedroom is stuck, and opening it sounds a little like knocking down a wall. It is nine thirty in the morning. She wanted to know what my schedule would be like for the day. Same as yesterday: cleaning my parents' house. She is on her way out and needs me to move my car. I guess it was time to get up anyway.

The cleaning continued. I came across my inoculation records, report cards, and baby photos, each one unique and never seen before. I was going so slowly; it was hard to stop myself from reading everything I came across.

I went into the city and back to the VIP room, hoping to see Cindy, but no such luck. I did, however, talk with this one woman, she called herself Minx. She had had a breast job. Her breasts were huge and looked like strange balloons. I was surprisingly attracted to her. The club was pretty empty. She walked over and asked me about myself. I found out she didn't have a boyfriend and was divorced. She lives with two men who protect her. Did she say she hadn't had sex in two years? I couldn't concentrate, and Cindy was nowhere to be found. I sucked down a scotch on the rocks and decided it was late enough to leave.

When I got out of the club, I noticed that my car wasn't there. Fuckin' New York, it had been towed. So, after one hundred and fifty dollars in impound fees, a seventy-five-dollar ticket, and a ten-dollar cab ride, I was back on my way to Lilly's. What a night. I need a vacation.

I crept inside the house and went to sleep crunched up in the shortened bed. Oh, in case I haven't described this before, let me take a moment to talk about the bed. It was short. My cousins, who used the bed when they were kids, had it when they were children, so it was a kids' bed. I could never completely stretch out. It drove me crazy. At the end of the bed were metal railings, which I would occasionally put my feet through.

I awoke to the sound of workers installing carpeting outside my door. It was time to get out of here.

I went back to Bayside to continue with the packing and cleaning. It was almost done. I decided to call it quits and go to the Nursing home to visit my mom.

My drive was on the Cross Island Expressway. It was the road I remembered most from my childhood. I was zipping along in my rent-a-wreck when, to my surprise, I got caught speeding. Shit, two tickets. The flashing lights were a definite awakening. As the cop walked over to me, he asked me, "What's the story with the car?" I guess it was apparent. I handed him my California driver's license and searched for the rent-a-wreck receipt.

As he walked back to his car, I mentioned that I was visiting my mom at the nursing home. I thought it couldn't hurt; perhaps he wouldn't give me the ticket. I sat in my car for what seemed like a long time. He made a gesture for me to come over to his car. Shit, what does he want? I slowly walked to his side; he gestured for me to go to the passenger side. He rolled down the window. OK, now what? It appears that I still had an outstanding ticket from 15 years ago, which had now turned into a warrant. He could arrest me, but since I was on my way to visit my mom, he was going to let me off with just the eighty-dollar speeding ticket. Boy, was I lucky. I drove away and then started to cry. Perhaps it was my brush with prison, maybe it was just the stress of seeing my life flash before me, or perhaps it was just my whole fuckin' life, but I cried. I continued my drive, trying to reassure myself that everything would be okay.

On the way over to visit my mom, I stopped at this Italian deli. Howard Beach was an old-world Italian neighborhood, filled with restaurants & good food. The deli wasn't too crowded, except for the occasional six-foot Italian goddesses that walked in.

My mom and I sat down to a lunch of corned beef and turkey in her room. She carefully spread the mustard on her sandwich and ate the whole thing. She had never done that before. After a while, it became difficult to engage in small talk, and we kept repeating the same subjects. I was tired. We ate watermelon. My mom carefully removed the seeds with the plastic knife. It was time to go; it had only been two hours, but I would be back. So, I said goodbye, told her I loved her, and then went back to the car, driving off.

Even though it was late, I felt the need to go into the city, although this time I just wanted to visit a café and hang out with the local coffee crowd. I missed the scene. What was New York going to be like? Who knew, but in any case, I figured I would find out. The action was now all on First Avenue—restaurant after restaurant filled with students and the eclectic bohemians from the New York scene.

I fit in perfectly. I went to a place called Alt Corner. It had all the elements of a great café: beat-up chairs, loud music, and cute girls sitting on the couch. I'll get back to them later. In any case, I walked right in and sat down at the counter. In the background, "The Who" was playing. "The Who," I thought. That is very different from what I would have expected. One of the guys behind the counter reminded me of an old friend that I still miss from Boston, Chris. It must have been 20 years since I last saw him. It was strange. This guy looked like him. There was a computer to my left, and when I went into the bathroom, I found more computers. It was odd. There was a bathtub filled with computers. They were piled up in the tub, about five feet high, in a very random fashion, with some urban art.

Summertime in New York. The café is warm and very moist. I go over to the sofa and sit down. My body is still killing me. Across from where I sit are the two gorgeous women I mentioned before. One girl has long, black hair; it is pulled up into a bun. She is wearing black army boots and is playing with some beads. She plays with them and then puts them on her wrist. She is wearing two barely visible shirts. The light white fabrics reveal a gorgeous body. Her friend across from her wears a black halter, and she is also wearing the beads on her wrists. It's an old couch that I'm sitting on. I'm slouching terribly, "The Who's": I'm free plays in the background. Suddenly… a brief blackout—everything stops. The girls sitting across from me say, "Blackout," and someone else in the café shouts, "First one of the season," and everything goes back to normal. It's late and I have that long drive back-shit, I hate that.

It's getting around time to leave New York and go back to Los Angeles.

Chapter 16 The Strip Club

Back in LA and at the strip club, I spent the evening talking to this very beautiful 21-year-old from Hawaii. Her name is Sky, and she initially walked over to me to try to get me to let her give me a lap dance. I said, "No," and she said, "Why not?" "Why?" Over and over, it went. She had this gorgeous, dark Creole complexion. I asked her what she thought of while dancing. We joked about all the different things she was thinking; certainly nothing any client would have guessed. Her father was Jewish, so I told her we would be a great match. I could tell my mom that I was going out with this nice Jewish girl.

Sky has a miniature chihuahua dog named "Mister." She told me that the dog liked to sleep with her on the bed. I said, "Who wouldn't?" She wouldn't stop laughing. It was great seeing her laugh—a kind of acceptance. Most strippers are very serious. I told her about my visit to the strip club in New York. She listened carefully as I described the floor setup and the dancer on the stage. I told her that the dancers in New York are not very good. They can't dance. They're awful. She loved that.

Of course, I dreamt of her last night. It was one of those warm, sensual ones. That kind that leaves you in one of those wistful moments. But she wasn't here, and I had to face my morning alone. Horny and alone.

Today was my first day of clinical training. Isn't that scary? Me as a therapist? Look out, psychos, I'm on alert. So, I got into my car and went over to the Clinic. We did three role-plays to see how we would each handle suicide, child abuse, and divorce. I played an angry, depressed man. After a few minutes, she stopped me. I didn't realize that I had all this anger inside of me. It was like acting again. What a surprise. I could feel the frustration of not being the actor I wanted to be. I promised myself that I would start acting again soon.

But first, I needed coffee and lots of it. I headed over to King's Road Cafe, where coffee is still a weapon. At King's Road, it was Mickey behind the counter; her short, sexy body was overflowing from her black slip. She leaned over to get my milk, and her perfectly shaped breasts were deep in my mind. "Breasts and milk, what a perfect combination," I thought. I think I have breast envy. I'll have to do more research on this subject.

TURNING FORTY

I decided to get a late lunch at Snarkali, a favorite Indian restaurant, but when I walked in, they were sleeping. Not just sleepy but sleeping in the booth.

I just came back from Ruth's wedding. Weddings are tough for singles. And this was worse: Abby was there. All those repressed feelings came to the surface. I'm a loser. I'm not married, and I don't even have a girlfriend. Forty and no girlfriend. Fuck. What happened? I mean, there were other women there besides Abby, but it was awkward. The time went very slowly. It was like having a cockblock everywhere I went.

I would sometimes flash back to my wedding fantasy. I imagined how proud my father would have been. I imagined all my relatives congratulating me. Instead, I am alone in this apartment. I could see him dancing and laughing, putting his arm on my shoulder, and giving me both ridiculous and insightful advice. I would never know this. I hate that

July 4th was a somewhat lackluster event. Instead of the usual fanfare, I just went over to Mucci's and hung out with the twins and their friends. I have to admit that the only odd thing that happened was when I went swimming. Mucci lives in a pad where Hunter S. Thompson once lived. It might have only been a few months, but he did live there. The ultimate bachelor pad, complete with a window looking into the inside of the pool. It features a studio with an unobstructed view of the entire valley. It is located down the block from one of Sharon Stone's residences and near where Michael Crichton lived. Every once in a while, when I am over there with my goggles, I swim down in front of the window, and you can see inside the studio. Mucci had it fixed up just perfectly. There was a couch in front of the windows, which filled the pad. There were drawings and paintings everywhere. There wasn't a window. The portal window always had a strange green color to it. It was slightly indented and about a foot and a half square.

TURNING FORTY

The pool was small but warm. There was a concrete fish sculpture that spewed water on one end and a small bridge on the other corner. The owner, an Oscar-winning director, occasionally wandered around with a glass containing whatever, most likely vodka; he was drunk. The rest of Mucci's pad was cluttered with glassware and books, except for the drafting table, which was situated to one side. That table was purchased because of a good day at the track.

Claudia and Kyra provided plenty of entertainment. They cooked the barbecue in the usual Mulholland manner: lots of sexiness and screaming at each other. After dinner, we looked through his video collection. The best we could come up with was "Double Indemnity"; truly a classic. We made it through most of it. That must be one of the all-time greatest movies, and anyone reading this who hasn't seen it should immediately stop and watch the movie. In any case, I headed home after the party.

Most of the work crew was at the VSDA show in Vegas, so the office had just a skeletal crew, which meant that by around two or three in the afternoon, I was ready to take off. But what always happens when you leave early? The boss calls. I wasn't more than five minutes away when I decided to check the machine to see if anyone had called. His message said, "Just checking, Marty. I wanted to see how things were going and what you're working on, etc." Fucking great. I pondered what to do as I approached the freeway and decided to risk going back to the office to call him and see if I could do a quick update and then cut out. Sure enough, I reached him in Vegas, where he was hanging out with our tattoo-encrusted CEO. The Internet world: can hardly wait till it's over. In any case, I reviewed the fifteen or so emails I had sent to different companies. I no longer do cold calling. That's way too eighties. Besides, who can stand the rejection? In any case, Fred then put the CEO in touch with those who wanted to congratulate me on getting this account.

Imagine that I've been in the Internet world for over a year, and I think I just made my first sale. One sale in fifteen months, that sucks. Anyway, I thanked him for his compliment, said goodbye, and immediately bolted to freedom.

I headed home to my insane apartment, where I quickly removed my sneakers and passed out for an hour. When I woke up, I realized it was time to go to yoga. I couldn't decide whether to go or not, even though I had this awful crick on my left side. But then I thought about all the yoga girls, and a minute later I found myself up and getting everything together. It's good I've got my priorities together: turning forty and loving it.

Yoga may be the answer to modern-day aches and pains. Just a few weeks in any yoga class and I'm sure you'll be feeling better. Monday. And you know how I feel about Mondays. Mondays. The crew is still out of town, and it's almost the end of the day. So, I cut out of work early again, at about four: not bad. But still it sucks. I don't know what I'm doing, not just in a deep sense, but that day-to-day stuff. I'm in Santa Monica. It's just like you'd expect; lots of sparsely clad women and cell phone-talking men. I start the new quarter at school tonight: Couples counseling. Unfortunately, I'm not in a relationship at the moment. Well, no romantic one, so I guess I'll have to store all that stuff in my head for later use.

Everything annoys me now, and I guess the fifty-minute drive to work doesn't help. I want to quit it all and go sell juice on the beach. Look for me in Hawaii, walking on the sand, slicing pineapples in half, and making Pina Coladas.

Finally, I am back in school, and it feels great. I am taking a class in Existential Psychology. Tonight's class shook me up. All that talk about "the Here and Now" and "Free Will" left me unsure of what to do first: quit my job or go on the road. What is the reason for our being? Is there a reason? Is there any meaning to life? Shit, all of that and I must go back to work tomorrow. But according to Existentialism, I could do whatever I wanted.

We talked about death and dying. If we had a real sense of how imminent our demise is, would we watch TV?

Would I? That is the question that comes up. I think about death more these days than ever before, and my existential class doesn't help.

I spoke to my mom again today. I try to call her every other day. I still don't know what to do. Was I the only person who talked to her? She kept on asking about my sister. "Oh, her, she's doing great. Yeah, we spoke the other day." What could I say? It was all so sad. There wasn't anyone I could share it all with, either. That certainly made it worse. My sister wasn't taking calls or making them. That's a nice way to deal with your sibling, and I guess it's not all that uncommon.

I'm hosting an art show this weekend, the first one in seven or eight years. The sharks will be in the show. I had been trying to do a little repair work on the big one. It's nine and a half feet. But working all day had fatigued me enough that I could barely get the plaster going. I had laundry to do, and I had to start packing. I had approximately two hundred pages to read for psychology, and I had to write a biography about myself. To make matters worse, Mister Big from the office, I mean the real Mister Big, all 300 million dollars' worth, was throwing a yacht party next Sunday, and I had to work at the clinic. I am missing a yacht party to take care of people with low incomes. Life sucks sometimes, ne pas?

I am at a different Starbucks, one close to where I work out in Woodland Hills. Nice neighborhood. The valley has its own weather system. It's always hot. It's just hot and sunny, like the desert it is. I need to fill out my application for the clinic. It's not an application, it's more like a review of my life: "Name the three most important moments in your life." That fits well with class last night, where they want us to write out what we'd like to see on our tombstones. I don't know. How about loser: "never really achieved what he wanted." Why bother? There is no real meaning to life anyway. I'm trying to stop drinking coffee. I guess that's not easy while I'm sitting at Starbucks.

Smoked a joint at lunchtime - well, it was three in the afternoon. I hadn't gotten high like this in four years. I called my mom from the parking lot at Starbucks. This time we talked for a long time, say twenty minutes. It was interesting to try to follow her logic. I was stoned. I tried to listen even more carefully. What does she mean by "how's your flowers?" She told me she had gone to the pool club but didn't go in. When I tried to contradict her, she asked me if I thought she was a liar. That was tough. But I hung in for a long time. Who else really talks to her?

The girls at Starbucks were up to their usual pattern of sharing stories about spilling and knocking over things. I had fallen in love with this one short, loud girl who had a cute Brooklyn accent. I flirted with her for a few minutes, then it was time to go.

Last night there was an art show. I have two sharks in the show. In the morning, I had a messenger pick up the big one and bring him to the gallery downtown. I must admit that the messenger was very surprised to see the shark. We carried the shark down the stairs, it wasn't that heavy, and when we got to his truck, he turned to me and said, "We're going to need a bigger truck. I was speechless and immediately flashed back to Jaws. It was a cinematic moment. He was Chinese, so it was somewhat difficult to understand what he was saying, but he kept repeating "giant shark" over and over.

The show was a hit, although I did arrive a little late. I had been to a BBQ earlier, so I was slightly burnt by the time I got there. But it was so good to be the shark man. I kept asking people as they stood underneath or to the side of the shark what they thought of it. "Oh, that's yours?" Women loved it, especially when they found out who I was, away from the beast. They would flash back to their moments of exhilaration and seem a little out of breath. One woman couldn't stop smiling at me. I went out after the show with Yvette, a local friend with an excellent sense of wit. Of course, I had met four other women that day—pretty good. I will follow up later this week.

After Yvette and I had a couple of drinks, I took her home, remembering that I still had some work to do for my clinical site the next morning. It was midnight. I headed to Swingers, one of the few places in LA where I could hang out and maybe get some work done. By the time I got there, it was almost one am. I began filling out the eight-page questionnaire. The girl behind the counter, wearing a short skirt, was Amy, who was also studying psychology. We bonded.

I was even more burnt than earlier, so I sucked down two cups of joe and started to pour my life story out in pen at Swingers. It took about forty minutes to complete. I thanked Amy and headed out. It was almost two; I had to be at the clinic, sober and ready to work, in 7 hours—oh the pain.

The clinical director reviewed with me all the dos and don'ts about being a therapist. They will project and transfer and have all sorts of ideas about you. You are not going out with them, entering into business with them, or meeting with them outside this clinic. She went on and on. I did notice a cute blonde in the waiting room. I guess I'll have to wait until I start seeing clients. And to think I thought that my friends would make good patients.

TURNING FORTY

Monday, and I was back in school, but today was a good day. I just returned from a couples counseling class. It's one of those classes that I wish I had taken first, but that's just how life is sometimes. Tonight was perfect—I volunteered to be a counselor. The teacher's name is Dr. Arthur and shit, he is good. I mean, when you have thirty years of experience, and you are still together, imagine how together you are. I was doing a role-playing with a couple. The wife wanted to go back to school. In any case, what do you do when your wife wants to do something new? I was not ready to go in front of the class, let alone sit next to Arthur. But I did it anyway. About five minutes into the role-playing, he stopped me and instructed me never to ask the couple how they were feeling about this or that, and instead, I was to discuss what the obvious feeling might be. You seem angry at what your wife is saying, or your wife seems dismayed at not being able to achieve her dreams. Anyway, there goes my whole method in one day. The rest of the session went better, and towards the end, I started to feel like a therapist. If he were my therapist, I'd probably still be in a relationship, although I'm not sure with whom exactly.

The rest of my Monday was not as exciting, although I must admit that my lunch at the Mongolian restaurant was odd. I think any restaurant in the valley that serves Mongolian food is most likely to be very different. In this place, they served us frozen meat. Then, we went up to a salad bar and added vegetables and other items. Further down was an oil bar. Frozen beef, now that is a little gross. There were various types of spicy oils, each with a sign indicating how to mix them to achieve a spicy or mild taste.

The end of a long day ended with my talking about death. Nobody talks about death. I reviewed my own death experience at the vodka bar.

I told the story in class about when my father died. It was hard to put it into words, but talking about it helped me.

The hardest thing about talking with my mom is trying to love her for who she has become, and trying to hold onto her for however long she has. It's painful to listen to her conversations that don't make sense. What do I say when she tells me that she got a new car or worked at an antique show? She would constantly ask about my father, and when he died, she would ask. So, I found myself repeating that he died four years ago, and yes, we buried him, and yes, there is a stone there. The energy to call my mom every day is enormous, but I don't want to stop. I do not want to abandon her.

Chapter 17 Existential class

I had my existential psychology class last night. But before class, I went over to Sebastian's and got stoned. I still can't believe I enjoy that. In any case, I couldn't talk for the first half hour, but then the death stories picked up the pace. We went around the room and talked about our dreams regarding death. Each one of us, or most of us, had had some death dream, and we went around the room sharing that experience. I shared my dream about seeing a dead body on the waterfront. I think it's from seeing too many Marlon Brando movies.

The great thing about the existential class is that there are a few gorgeous women in the class. My favorite is Sondra. She is 23, tall, blonde, friendly, and has blue eyes, of course. After each class, I walked her to her car, and we talked for about half an hour. All I could do was think about having sex with her as we talked on and on about death. Weird? But I could have spoken to her about socks, and it would have turned me on. I told her that if she ever had a nightmare, she could call me. "Don't worry," I said, "call me any time." She told me that I could call her. I fantasized about calling her with some terrible nightmare and having her come over, or better yet, driving over to her place to lie down next to her. I invited her to see the shark, and we said goodnight. No kiss, shit, well we are classmates.

Packing and moving twice in one summer was way too much work. I walked into my crammed and semi-packed apartment and realized that I was too tired to do anything except drink a quart of pea soup. I think it's comfort food for me. I slowly got up off the couch and passed out in bed. I still must get the boxes out of the car trunk.

It has been seven years since I moved last, and I estimate there must be at least a hundred boxes of junk to pack. I guess I'll be up late tonight.

I had one of those mornings when the clock moved ever so slowly. We ate Chinese food at eleven, so you know the day was going badly. I tried to keep focused, but all I wanted to do was to go outside and get stoned. I snuck out but needed to get some papers, so I went to the head shop. There, behind the counter, was this very lush-looking woman named Francesca. Her big eyes and warm smiled fucked me up. Her beautiful cleavage was driving me crazy. But I held on and only asked her to get something from a lower shelf three times. I was in love, and it was only noon.

I escaped from the head shop and moved over to Starbucks for some iced coffee. I sucked that down quickly and hit the road to get high. I was driving for about five minutes. It must have been 105 outside, and the AC in the Beemer was out. After taking a few hits, I passed this wonderful woman hitchhiking. I, of course, noticed that her bag was small, no room for a gun, so I decided to pick her up. Her tight mini dress was quite visual, skintight, etc. This was the first time I can ever remember picking up a hitchhiker.

Rene sat down in my car, and I quickly started a conversation. She was a local, and she claimed to be on disability. She was charming. Every few minutes, I would turn my head to get a glimpse of whatever part I could. She was friendly. All I wanted to do was have sex with her. I didn't know where to take her or what to do. She told me she had been adopted, that she had a lot of anxiety. I could see that she had bitten her nails. I held her hand. She didn't flinch. She told me she was borderline. What? I asked her what caused her anxiety. She laughed and said to me that I shouldn't ask her such questions. Whatever. She told me that she had lost her job, that her car was broken, and that her cell phone was turned off. But she didn't ask me for money. I kept driving; my car was so fuckin' hot it was annoying. All I wanted to do was pull her closer. But that never happened. Instead, I took her to a local bar where she had worked. I don't remember the name of the bar, but it was something like "Sweet Treats." We sat down amongst all her local friends and had a drink.

This bar was the kind that you might expect in the valley in the middle of the day, a kind of barfly environment. Everyone

knew Rene. But that was OK. They were all drunk, especially
that guy with the large red nose sitting next to her. The girls on
the side kept saying, "She's a nice girl. Make any guy happy." It
was as if I had met her extended family. I didn't know what to
do. I had to go back to work, although in retrospect, I could have
spent more time with her. I asked her for a number, and after
borrowing the pen from the barmaid, she wrote it down on the
back of an ATM receipt. She said… "I'm busy the next few days,
but maybe lunch next week." She smiled. I put my hand on her
shoulder and took off. When I got back to the office, I tried the
number. It said that the number wasn't accepting calls. Maybe
after her disability check clears, we will see. A few days later, it
was disconnected. I guess we shall never meet again.

Perhaps I'm not the only one who moves in the middle of
the summer, but it seemed like that. I woke up Friday with that
feeling of dread that only a very long and arduous weekend
could bring. Saturday was to be the day I moved. Imagine
moving after eight years. My apartment, like my parents, was
cluttered with tons of stuff. I mean, I had lived there for a long
time, and there were so many books, papers, shoes, and art—lots
of art. I carefully packed up all 60 or 70 boxes, although not
carefully. Then I called the movers. Wouldn't you know that I
ended up with friendly Jewish boy movers? Funny, it was three
guys from Mexico who moved me in. But that was on Saturday.

Friday night was the final night of my first art show. The
sharks were on sale. I showed up late; it was after all downtown
LA. I hadn't been in downtown LA for a long time. Well, except
for the opening night of the show. This was the closing ball. I
don't know about "a ball," but anyway. I had invited quite a few
friends, and in the end, Ben and his wife came, as did Chuck and
Marla, and Sebastian and Abby (a different Abby).

I ran into Ben as I was parking. Ben is the Director of
Technology at the office. He was one of those computer guys who

could seemingly fix anything. I loved that. He was there with his wife from England, who did horoscope charts. I will have her do mine later. Anyway, he moved his car so I could park. Downtown LA is not very hospitable, but I guess people experiencing homelessness work it out.

Inside the gallery, the show was already going on. Tyler and his cronies greeted me. They were doing performance art in the shark room. I took out the video camera and started to shoot again. I videotaped the shark from as many angles as possible. Anyway, there was a lot of music and people dancing around. Bob also showed up; he was an old friend of Chuck's. The evening went fast. I talked to as many people as I could. It wasn't as fun as the opening. It had that post-show depression. The artists were removing their unsold pieces, which needed to be put back into the car.

I stayed around for a little while. The sharks were waiting for the show to begin. That was good, since it was Friday and I was moving on Saturday, so not having to move 12 feet of shark was a very good thing. I didn't go out after the show. I just went home and continued to pack.

I was late for the packing scene. Even the 'pack and move' sign didn't work, but I had bought 30 boxes, so I knew the move would happen. However, I must say that I couldn't believe it was after eight and a half years that I was moving out.

I woke up early and went over to Swingers for breakfast. The music was blasting at 7 am. I once made the mistake of asking them to lower the music. Their response was, "That is why people come to Swingers." Oh, I see. Got to love that. The one waitress who was working was, as they all are, lovely. They made them wear short skirts; I think the boots were optional. I ate quickly and then went back home. The movers arrived and began the task of emptying the apartment. It was a lot of work, and I paid $90 an hour. After four and a half hours, they were ready to go to the new place. It was in Los Feliz, an ancient part of the Hollywood scene. It features two bedrooms, is significantly quieter, and has just been freshly painted, with hardwood floors. This was the Red Apartment.

It was time to say goodbye to Detroit Street. That had quite a long legend, I'd been there since '92, shit; a long time. I moved there to be closer to my favorite café, "the pick-me-up." The café had closed a long time ago. Many girlfriends have seen this place, with lots of parties—a whole other life. My parents were both alive when I moved in there. This was posted by Kandy, though. The last girlfriend was before I moved in here.

The move went well, and after buying the crew lunch and paying them $700, I was settled in the new pad.

Even though I was exhausted after the move, I went to the twins' birthday party. They were celebrating their 30th birthday and were planning a party that would be equally big. It was at Elan's house. He is an ER doctor. The funny thing was I asked him for a Band-Aid, and he didn't have one. Could that be possible, or was he just busy hitting on all the girls in his pad? Nothing like watching a player at work.

My legs were chaffed from moving all day. As I walked, I had a little hop. Mucci mentioned it to me after we walked to the store. It looked like I had been riding a horse. I left around 11 pm since I had to wake up early.

Sunday, and I had my first client at the clinic. I was a trainee therapist. I was very nervous, so I arrived early, around 8:30. I quickly reviewed the charts and intake forms. I can't reveal much due to confidentiality. I was exhausted. But here was my first client. I was so nervous that I had to run to the bathroom before seeing him.

Bernard walked into the room very calmly and sat in the large chair. I sat across from him. It was a fifty-minute session. I looked at the clock. Ok, so I said, "What is it you want to work on?" Then we went through his whole life. It was exhausting, but I listened carefully. After a few minutes, I noticed that my fly was open. Wait, did you get that? My fly was open. Shit, what was I going to do? I was paralyzed. I didn't know what to do first. Should I pull it up or leave it down? I crossed my legs every which way I could. I wanted to stand up and walk around, but I couldn't move. Then it was time to wrap up, so I waited until he stood up, then carefully stood up, turned, and zipped my fly. He told me he wanted to come back. My first client... with my fly down. Doesn't life suck sometimes?

After the session, we went into supervision. There, I got to review the whole story, except for the fly. I was so tired that after that, I went into one of the rooms assigned to patients and lay down on the soft couch, pulled up a pillow, and relaxed in the cool, air-conditioned room for 50 minutes. I slept well.

It was so peaceful. I hope I wasn't snoring too loudly. It was time to go home to the new place. My new apartment was still unpacked, and I wasn't prepared to undertake the challenge.

I have been meeting with this company regarding a new opportunity, so my day was spent wondering if they would call or not. I went out last night with my boss, as if anyone was my boss, and it was odd to tell him that I was thinking about this other gig. He was so lovely that I must admit that I felt a little guilty. We attended one of those unusual Hollywood award shows. This one was a celebration between the Internet and video rentals.

I found myself talking to this one woman wearing a shiny evening dress and carrying a cane. She told me about having her babies stolen by the South Americans and that they murdered her husband. "Very odd," I thought, and I quickly moved over to the bar. I mean, I'd like to know more about that. I don't think so.

I quickly moved over to the bar. There, I met two women from Universal who were hoping to win for the best home page: how mundane. They got their drinks first; all the alcohol was free till eleven. I ordered a scotch that was twelve dollars. Twelve dollars? Carol, the girl from Universal, asked, "How come so much?" "Oh, don't worry, I said- I'm a millionaire." Women love that line. We talked for a while. I can't even remember where they were from. That's one of the first questions I ask someone. Where are you from? It tells a lot. In any case, we walked through the crowded bar. I paused and watched Fred talking to the woman in the shiny dress. I was waiting to see the expression on his face when she told him about the kidnapping and the aliens. Then we walked into the room where these Internet awards were being announced. Universal didn't win, and the girls took off. Carol, this one cutie, paused for a second before leaving. I was going to ask her for her number, but everything moved too quickly, and before I knew it, she was gone forever. I had given them my card, but women never call you first unless: 1) you are a millionaire, 2) a big Hollywood agent, 3) remind them of their father, 4) they are well... you figure it out.

I walked over to find Fred, my partner or boss, as they are known. Doesn't that suck when someone can call themself your boss? I hate that. Fuck that. He got plastered. The party was continuing in that usual style: drunken chicks on the dance floor with drunken guys watching from the side. The night was quickly fading, and my apartment, filled with boxes, was waiting for me.

I received an offer from my new job while I was at work today. Finally. Getting out of Woodland Hills.

I just came home from my Existential class. I feel so meaningless. Life sucks. I am alone. All alone. Utterly alone. I create my universe. I am what I produce. Doesn't that sound cheery? It's all about the here and now, not the then and there.

I feel better. I am going to quit my job on Friday. I'll get my check for two grand and tell them it's a wrap. I can hardly wait. It's a good thing to change jobs and apartments. It does add a little newness to my otherwise hectic life. Before I moved to LA people would ask me what it was, I was going to do: "get an apartment, a job and a car. Then get a bigger apartment, a better job and a better car, then a two bedroom, a great job and a killer car," etc., etc., etc.

Chapter 18 Al Gore

I had three clients last Sunday. I'm not sure about being a therapist. It's a tough gig; all those problems. At the end of the weekend, all I could think of was that I now had not only my problems to deal with but also everyone else's. Shit, that's hard. I mean, especially when you get into real issues. I would hold on and try to be as supportive as possible. "Hey, good job," "that's tough," and the infamous "you're doing a lot of great work." It was hard to focus for the hour that I was there. But no matter what, I stayed with each one, and that was very tiring.

TURNING FORTY

I had another opening last Thursday. Now that was a lot of fun. I stood near the sharks and just asked people what they thought of them. I met Naomi, Marjory, Nikki, and Honey. Quite a crew, Honey, especially. She was wearing a tight blue dress. I just wanted to grab her. She had these great breasts. I love art. But I think I'm falling in love with Naomi. Her short red hair made me think about running through it. I resisted the temptation, and I foolishly did not get her number. Oh, and then there was Mary from Universal. She was wearing this very light reddish shirt with a large circle in the middle. This revealed her beautiful, pert breasts. I resisted the temptation. She was charming. We talked for a while, and then she left. I tried to get her number. But all I could do was give her mine, and you, that never works.

What could be worse than having to take the Beemer in for repairs? I had been thinking of ways of getting out of work and Beverly Hills BMW is always filled with babes, lots of beautiful pissed off babes. I guess they like Beemer's. This lovely woman was wearing a see-through white lace top. I said a couple of one-liners, and then she walked away. It's always such high drama there; it could easily be a sitcom.

It is now Thursday, the day Al Gore is accepting the democratic nomination and, I thought, my last day at work in the valley. I took yesterday off, so today I got called into Fred's office and railed with questions. I squiggled and libbed my way through. I even cracked a few jokes; I'm leaving anyway, why not have a little fun?

Al Gore promised to make every school "gun-free." He sounded good. Just imagine if the world had a leader —someone who was big enough to affect the planet and small enough to do it right.

TURNING FORTY

So, I'm going to quit my job tomorrow. Finally, after eight months and countless days, it will come to an end. I can hardly wait to leave. I'll wait until after I get my paycheck and a massage by Karen, the" Mary Kay dancer massage therapist." Then I'll grab him for a few minutes in his office and come up with a memorable speech to quit and shift some of the blame to some unknown force. In any case, I'm sure it will be quite a moment when I drop the bomb. I'm getting too old to go through jobs.

The week was very odd, and I counted the seconds waiting to quit. Now, a week later, it's been an extraordinary experience, having counted each day at work. Quitting a job is one of the most freeing experiences. I'll do it after the massage, I figure, this way I'll be relaxed and then a little tense. Oh, and of course, I'll have gotten paid. Doesn't it suck to be so worried about money? And all I want to do is act.

What is it about turning forty that has made everything look different? It must be death anxiety. We all start to count the years differently; we are closer to death than to birth, well, unless we live past eighty. Knowing the end is coming has to make things more difficult, yet it should also be easier.

OK, so today was going to be my last day at work. You know the plan; I was going to wait 'til after the massage and then get my check and then quit. However, after distributing checks at 10 am for five years, they decided to change the policy today. I nearly died when I found out. So, I sweated there at my desk. Fred called me into his office and made me review accounts. At one point, I almost quit. I moved all the papers onto the other chair. I was going to stop reviewing the big plans for our future and then just quit. But then he got a phone call, and all I could think of was, "Stick to the plan." While all of this was going on, my tooth began to feel like it was time for a root canal. Moreover, there was also that streaming pain.

Fred and I reviewed several companies, and he made a call that successfully reached Atom Films regarding the deal we were trying to finalize. In any case, all I could do was think about how I was going to get my check, cash it, and quit, all within three hours. It was going to be tight, but what the hell? So, when the checks came, I went to the bank and deposited most of them. Then I went back thinking, "Well, why worry? I am going to quit anyway." But much to my surprise, Fred was out, and so I waited. By four thirty, he still wasn't back. Cynthia, Fred's assistant, wouldn't tell me right away whether he was coming back or not. As I waited, I began to clean out my desk and files, being careful not to draw attention to myself. Suddenly, the phone rang, and it was our CEO, the ex-hippy, tattooed lawyer. He had dialed my number by mistake, and of course, I answered the phone, my mind elsewhere. He wanted to speak with the finance representative. That was weird. Sometimes they check my emails and other forms of communication, but I will let it go. In any case Fred never returned so I will have to wait 'til Monday to quit, shit.

One more thing to complain about. I received a letter from Reemus, the company that managed my old apartment, with a bill for $ 230. Did you understand that? Not only was I not getting my security back, but I also owed them money, those bastards. I fantasized about picketing the front of the office and plastering posters about how they rip people off everywhere. Someone ran the company, but I certainly never got his name. It all seemed so shady.

I called the accountant and asked him to refund all the money. OK, maybe I didn't leave the apartment that clean, but still, well... and maybe there were lots of holes in the walls from the sharks and other pieces of art. But still, and perhaps I left some trash and a few broken windows, isn't it amazing how they have the nerve to try and rip me off like that?

I met with the crew last night at the Conga Room. Boy, there are tons of ladies just dying to dance. The best part, though, had to be my friend's father, a 55-plus accountant who danced up a storm. At one point, he was cheek to cheek with this very sexy blonde, wiggling and mamboing around the floor. I could hardly believe my eyes. It was very inspirational. Mental note: must make the most of life.

Since I'm in a new neighborhood, I decided to check out one of the many local strip clubs. What a surprise. It was very lackluster. I guess I had become so used to women walking around naked at the other club, and this was very conservative. They were hardly naked at all.

Today is the day I am going to quit my job. It is about 8:20 in the morning, and I linger at home. It's good to be at work on time on the day you're going to quit. It adds to the drama. "It was just an ordinary day. He was in on time," they would say. "Something must be wrong. He is never on time. That day he was."

I'm just going to give him a letter of resignation. That's a huge, dramatic thing to do. Then, just silence, and then hand him the letter, and think to myself, "I am quitting this piece of shit job." Let the music from "I'm Free" play in my head. Have a medley of songs on freedom playing. Then play hardball about getting out and splitting. It's a wrap, finally, after eight arduous months. It's over, yes.

I have been sitting too long in my apartment typing, and now I'm going to be late. Shit, being late on the day you quit, well, I've got to go.

So, I just did it. I quit, and this is how it all went down. I arrived late at work, and when I got there, Fred was already at work. So, I had to wait 'til around ten to eleven. I then walked into his office with two messages. One was a referral for a licensing deal. So first I handed him that note, then I waited for a beat, and then said, " I have something else for you. I then handed him the letter of resignation. I had written "letter of resignation" on the top portion, like it was a title. I did not want there to be any mistakes. The letter said: "in the last few weeks it has become apparent to me that my interests lie outside my current position I am therefore submitting this letter of resignation." He jumped when he came to that part of the letter. I just smiled. We talked about the new job for a while. I told him that they wanted me to start right away. I wanted to leave that second, but he convinced me to stay through the week. That was it. It was over. I was moving on, and I could hardly believe it. Yes. I went back to the cubicle and did not know what to do next. I mean, I hardly worked before. What am I going to do now? Well, I did need new tires, so it was off to the tire store, always a good thing to do in the middle of the day. I did not tell anyone. I was curious how long it would take and who would be the first one to say something. It was like in "The Godfather," The traitor would try to set the meeting. I was going to sit back and wait and see what happened.

Anyway, I guess this is going to be one of my last times at Starbucks in the valley.

There is something odd about some people out there, and I mean "out there." I was on my way to my Existential class when I drove by this very young, beautiful woman crying on the side of the road in Santa Monica. At first, I couldn't stop, but then I drove around the block a second time to more thoroughly investigate. There, I met Yahve; she was from Spain, or at least that is what she said to me. I wasn't sure what to do. "What's wrong?" I asked naively. She walked over to my car, so I offered her a ride. She was terrific, with big blue eyes. She is on my couch at this moment. Anyway, nothing else is going on, but I spent all night listening to her stories about little beings and the alternative universe. At one point, I thought she was so crazy that I might want to take her to the psych ward, or better yet, that maybe she had escaped from the ward. It was all bizarre. And I got sucked into it and that was the only thing that got sucked in. She resisted all my temptations and stuck me with a bill for a bottle of wine, sushi, and five dollars. Five dollars? A cheap date at that.

I was a little nervous about letting her sleep in the living room while I slept in my bed. I thought she might kill me while I slept, so I slept on the rug in the living room. At about 4:00 a.m., she woke up and went into the bedroom. I followed. She did not remove one stitch of her clothes. She was even wearing my favorite fuzzy red sweater. I made her remove the shirt before she left. It was a cold thing to do, but I hadn't been laid in a while, and it was my favorite sweater—end of story. Besides, the girl in Chicago stole the black one and I was still pissed about that.

This was all in preparation for our trip to New York. I wasn't quite sure why I was going, but I knew that I had to go. I arrived on a rainy and humid August 30th, 2000.

Right now, I'm sitting at Café Orlins, one of my original old haunts in New York. I think I'm sitting at the table where I met TJ sixteen years ago. I think it was on a Wednesday that I met her, after my acting class. She was one of my first lovers. She has since disappeared back into the universe.

"Café Orlins is like the 'pick me up' was in LA. I spent one whole summer just sitting, eating pasta, gorgonzola, and drinking iced lattes. Last year, when I was visiting, I tried to order the pasta, and they just looked at me like I was from another planet. "Pasta Gorgonzola," I had never heard of it. The waitress must have been in her twenties; she would have been about five years old when I last ordered it. Don't you hate that when they stop serving your favorite dish? Well, I ordered the hummus —an alternative that I used to enjoy, but it just wasn't the same.

I was back on cleanup duty in Bayside, and I must admit that I'm not doing very well. I walked into the apartment, looked around like a visitor, and then left. It was only when I realized that I had not done any real work that I forced myself to go back and take out three bags of clothes for donation. That sucked.

I then went to the country club that we used to visit. I had to go there to sell the membership. It brought back way too many memories. I walked through the gate and started to look around. I was flashing back between time and moods. I had grown up using that pool. Inside the office, there was this one adorable blonde. She was mainly in another zone. I tried to strike up a conversation, but it didn't go anywhere. The woman I was dealing with pulled out the file, and there it was: the four original photos of the happy family. My lower lip was hanging incredibly low. I remembered my dad always putting his finger under my lip to help my overbite. The photos were from 1965. I, of course, asked if I could keep them. She agreed, and I was off. But before I could leave, I had to take a complete walk around. I went to the snack bar to remember their egg rolls. I then walked past the kiddie pool, but it was no longer there. Instead, there was a small playground. I went into the men's locker room and went over to my old locker, number 266. I opened the door, almost expecting to find something, but to no avail; it was empty. I then took an intense breath and split. The end of an era. Lots of summers spent there. I wanted to take a dip in the pool. It looked good and there were plenty of bikinis surrounding the area, but all I had on were some lousy briefs, so I left. Farewell, pool club, thanks for the memories, I'll miss you.

Chapter 19 School again

I'm back in LA and started my new job today. Imagine that I got a new job after eight months of complaining. I finally started a new gig.

I am Director of Business Development. There are two hot women in the office—one works as a receptionist, and the other works in development upstairs. I made half a dozen calls, and one was a local DP that the company had initially hired and then fired. So, I called him and pitched the idea. It was a comedy of errors.

The team of boys all went out to lunch. Two of the guys were from out of town, somewhere in Europe. Swiss investors provided the company's funding. Are we getting paid in chocolate? The team visited a small French café in Venice. It was right next to Pilates' place, so there were tons of women. It was an "HBC," otherwise known as high babe count. Let me add that we could also have had a "LBC" or low babe count, or "EHBC," extremely high babe count, could be dangerous, or of course, MBC, mid babe count.

I reviewed all the business models I could find. I was leading the team, and it was tough to keep it going.

But it was a new job, and it was in Venice. The drive was in the other direction, heading west. I went down Venice Blvd. I was at the beach, and that's what counted. No more Woodland Hills and The Valley, excellent.

After work, I had my Existential class. It was time to go up and do my presentation—the one I was supposed to give when I met Yahve. I had written a paper on a chapter in Love's Executioner. Slowly, I hacked my way through it. It was all intense stuff. The chapter was about a shrink and how we never truly know why people react in a certain way, even when we think we understand.

Day 2 at the new job. We have six months to make the company happen. I called Danielle, the girl from my old job, who was very cute and had shown some interest in me. I had been sending her emails since I left. I found out that she never received the emails, as they had instead gone to the VP of Finance. He was reading all my love notes. Now, that's funny.

I received a voicemail from a patient of mine who is in crisis. Her rent was going up. Just pay it and move on. How odd, huh? Can't she get it together?

Otherwise, most of the day was spent talking about footage. I spoke with a man who had the most extensive footage library of bald eagles. But the best part had to be seeing Lynette, the girl in development, again. She was wearing a cute red top with gray pants. Her toenails were painted a sparkly red polish. She would walk upstairs, across from me. Our eyes would meet, and she would smile. I could feel my blood heat up. I wonder how old she is. She handed me a list of categories for the archive. I thanked her. I laughed when I looked at the list of 150 items. Was he kidding? Sure, I could put that together for a few million. Lynette walked away. I followed her whenever I could as she walked around the office. We exchanged smiles all day. How perfect people seem when we first meet them.

Last night in my Existential class, for some reason, I asked about this couple I was seeing. What do you do when there is a problem with the relationship? Separateness," she declared, and suggested that they find as many different things to do apart as possible. It is all about individuating.

A brutal day at the clinic. My supervisor grilled me to the point where all I wanted to do was to say… "fuck you… What are you deaf? Can't you hear me?" She kept asking, "So what was the presenting problem?" The presenting problem is that they both want to kill each other. Isn't that enough? I'm not familiar with this counseling business. It's not easy, in case you were wondering. I did not know what to say to the couple either. Listen, try to be nice to each other. Look, it is neither of your fantasies. The dream is over. This is reality. Surprised? Shit, what the fuck can I do?

Now I have to write two papers: one ten pages long, the other six. Wish me luck. There's nothing like being back in school again.

I am thinking that if I use a larger font for the paper, it might go quicker. So, I used fourteen; well, whatever. I am done.

The quarter has ended. I am genuinely sick of school. But it is September 11, 2000. September has always symbolized the beginning of the school year to me. It smells like back at school.

The paper is done. The class is over. It was such a great class, the last Existential class. It started with that slow-talking guy, Ted, going over the meaninglessness. This is the point in existence when you realize that there is no meaning to life. We all went around the room. I read from the beginning of my paper. Here it is:

How could anyone think of using Nietzsche as a character in a book? Of all the writers in history, he exudes one of the largest senses of isolation and of asking to be left alone. But then again, Yalom includes Sigmund Freud, whom he has taken to calling Sig as well. Throw in the infamous Anna O and some existential innuendos, and you have a compelling psychological novel, "A Novel of Obsession" as it is called. In the end, Bertha is purged from Breuer's soul, Nietzsche returns to his life, Sig declares it was just a cigar, and the family has a happy conclusion.

That's how it came out. Is there meaning to life? Not really. It is only what we create. We all think about death. It is our death anxiety. We must strive for freedom, and we are all isolated from one another. Great.

Day five of starting a new company. We have been collecting emails to do an extensive campaign. That is my plan: to keep sending out enough emails 'til something happens. I said in a press release that after you send in the footage, sit back and wait for the cash to roll in. The V. Cs loved that, I'm sure. They have been sending emails for days. I told them, let's try for seventy-five thousand, but five thousand would be an excellent start.

We are moving to a new office tomorrow. A new temporary one. Another move, I am starting to feel like a gypsy. Then we will move again. The funny thing today was running into my teacher from the existential class. I went there with Leon, someone I used to eat lunch with every day. It is one of those cycles in life.

The new office is made of glass and black metal. It has a high-tech, gothic vibe. There is a large water sculpture in the lobby. It has the appearance of glass, as the water cascades carefully off the top. There were also other people moving in. I mentioned that I was thinking of putting a goldfish in the fountain. They imagined sea snakes. Well, whatever. Goldfish next week.

I didn't get any work done today. I received an email in response from a company that might be interested, but nothing else has happened since then. I called Abby, though, and left a message. She called me back and left two messages. Well, whatever.

The 2000 Olympics featured some of the most impressive lighting, particularly during the torch ceremony. The flame starts in water in Sydney. There is water everywhere. There is a waterfall going down the side of the stadium. The cauldron of fire slowly edges its way up. It looks like a flaming flying saucer.

Okay, so here's another romance story. Mandy, a friend from San Diego, is a soon-to-be divorced 31-year-old mom. She is a total babe. She has a killer body, even though she had this kid two years ago. I first saw her wearing a see-through tan dress with a bikini underneath. It was quite a scene. My eyes nearly fell out of my head. I tried to control myself when, later, I was lying next to her on the soft sands of the Malibu shore.

Later that evening, we all went back to her house to take showers. I could have tried to get an orgy going but it was a husband-and-wife team. Her mother had been a famous movie star in the 40s. It all made sense. I was disappointed that I did not take her number. I don't know what's wrong with me sometimes. She also breastfed her daughter at dinner. That made for an interesting moment. Ah, lucky child. But I could see the mother was a little annoyed. She had been sick as well and looked a little tired. That's a tough job, raising a child. Indeed, it is harder than I work.

I went swimming after work at Mucci's pad. He has got two weeks left, and then he is out. The killer pad is gone. No more summer parties around the pool. No more twins on the grill.

It is one fifteen in the morning and I am fuckin' wide-awake sitting on my couch, which is not too good considering it is Monday night. Well, whatever. Who sleeps anymore? I have a slight toothache, so I took Vicodin. That sounds right. Can you imagine what it would be like if I had a migraine?

The night is a tough time for some people. They reiterate their life in their mind, never letting go of worries. Do not be like that. Just try to relax. Change the tapes running inside your head. Get right on it.

I called my old job today and found out that they laid off twelve people last Friday. I got out at the right time. How funny. Cynthia, Fred's assistant, is also gone, as is the number two guy, a man who looks more like an Alien than anyone in Men in Black I know. He is gone. Well, that is the Internet.

I was wondering what to write about. I could describe going out last night with this tightly wound friend of Diana's, but I might as well explain how my car got totaled today. I was cruising along when this huge Ford Expedition truck, making a left into my lane, smashed into my side. It sent me speeding onto the sidewalk in front of "American Burger." What a fuckin' nightmare. Lucky, I walked away. Now that is a near-death experience. The car went up the handicapped ramp on the corner. Fortunately, there was no one standing at the corner, or I surely would have nailed them. It is a miracle, I think. The people who were behind me were amazed that I managed to skate up the sidewalk like I did. The car had brand new front Michelins. They cost one fifty each. Remember when I got them? After the accident, I was in shock, and even though the whole left side was smashed in, all I could do was scream at the guy for ruining my new tires. Ok, mental note, I must take a vacation soon.

I went to see an Attorney today. Of course, I hired an attorney. I mean, this is Los Angeles, and I was in an accident.

I've just finished counseling day. I saw four clients and I have got to say, people are fucked up out there. My thoughts on couples are that there are some central truths, much like the four ultimate concerns regarding existentialism, but different. The first is that all women want their guy to be more prosperous. So, hey, you guys out there, better get used to it. If the women are making more than you, you are most definitely in trouble. The second truth is that all men will let their wives or girlfriends take care of them for the rest of their lives if given the opportunity. The third is that no one likes to clean, so hire a housekeeper. The fourth is that men are not overly romantic, and training is always essential. The fifth is that all women want their men to change, and that all men want their women to stay the same. The sixth truth is that all women want their guys to dance with them, especially at a wedding. At the very least, hold them and sway back and forth. You might not win any contests, but you will make the girl happy. The seventh is that you must work on yourself, regardless of the circumstances; that is your job.

My couple started the session today with her crying. That was tough. She just cried and cried, and then I began to find out what was going on between the two of them. I never knew that they both had had affairs. How is that for some news? She was even supporting the child—imagine that! I was surprised to hear that she was trying to prevent him from going out with his friends. I listened as she described how this bothered her. I think all guys, at times, just want to hang out with the thugs- it's just so much easier. The wife did not like that. And then she cried some more. I thought enough already. I'm not familiar with this clinic; it's much tougher than I thought.

It's Sunday, and I have work tomorrow as usual. I have more appointments, including an eye doctor appointment, and then some client visits. On Friday, a bunch of us went to this little Mexican dive restaurant after work. It was Marena's last day at work. The whole crew was there, including the Swiss contingent. I hate sitting at the table with the bosses. It isn't enjoyable. You do not know what to do or what to say. "Better to keep it quiet," I thought.

On Saturday, I went over to "the Good Luck bar." Working on Sunday makes it hard to party Saturday night, but I tried my best. I strolled around the bar. It is always crowded on Saturday, and then I ran into a group of three girls. The one I met a woman named Linda, and she was wearing braces. "Braces, how cute," I thought. Her cleavage was so intense that all I wanted to do was grab, but I resisted. It was hard. I bought the three of them drinks, and her two girlfriends left us alone. We talked about salsa dancing. I offered to take her out to this expensive dance club right down the block from where I used to live. "Money, oh, do not worry about that. I am a millionaire," I would say. Of course, picking her up in my rented Taurus might not be the best way to seduce her, but I could always rent another rental car. All I could do was look at those breasts and think to myself, "slow dancing and wild sex," but look out for the braces. They were going to go to a party in Sylmar." Where the fuck is Sylmar?

I thought to myself. I need a girlfriend. Linda was living with her parents and going to Valley College. I want to go to Valley College. Imagine how much fun that could be. Do you think I am too old?

She wrote down her number on a red napkin, and the three of them took off—a number. "Not bad," I thought, and they must have carded her, so she must be at least 21— "perfect," I thought. I wandered around the bar a little and then decided to go over to the strip club. I was so horny, and I did not know what to do. Cheetahs were in walking distance, so I strolled my ass over there to see what was going on. It was the usual vibe; not nearly as lovely as the club on La Cienega, but there were women, and that helped, although you can be sure that I didn't get any. Oh, and it was Rosh Hashanah, the Jewish New Year. So, Happy New Year.

Chapter 20 Riding in Elevators

Well, they hired a new girl at the office today: this friendly woman from Italy. She was thin, wearing tight pants, expensive black shoes, a tight yellow shirt, and large-framed dark glasses, her smile wide and bright. I could see her diagonally across from my desk inside my office. She spent the day reading the script for the movie they were going to shoot. She was married to someone incredibly famous. She was our international salesperson. Reminds me of Romana, that beautiful Czech woman. I walked by her several times. I will have to take her out for lunch. Otherwise, it was just another day in paradise.

They had the first presidential debate tonight. I had a scheduling conflict. I was sorry that I couldn't make it. The debates were broadcast on TV in the schoolroom. It was also the first night of my "Treatment of Borderlines" class, what an appropriate coincidence.

My schedule was hell now, and so each week went by in that land of oblivion. I dreamt of a simpler life, a life with some fuckin' meaning, but there was none. Instead, I just languished in my moments of self-pity and disgust. I didn't know what to do, and yet I thought I would, but I found myself repeatedly struggling, which was exhausting.

I met with the thugs last night over at the Sunset Strip row of restaurants. That was great. We spent time together for a while, snacking on food and watching as the pretty girls strolled past us. Mucci told stories of his new house, and I sat by thinking of all the money I had wasted over the years. Lamont called me on the cell phone in the middle of one of our group moments. He mentioned that there was this great jazz sax player over at the Bel Age hotel. After finishing all the food, we headed over to see what was up.

I had forgotten about Mucci's anxiety about going in elevators, so we had to find the stairs. There were just a few women at the hotel. On the table to our right sat a wonderful woman wearing black gloves, eating shrimp. Imagine that: eating shrimp wearing gloves. It did seem a little odd. We stayed for a little while and then took off. Mucci wanted to get back home, and I wanted to go to the party.

Kings Road had the usual assortment of weird individuals. Then, suddenly, Sandy walked over to me. Her deep eyes and warm smile were captivating, not to mention her stunning physique. I read a page of the book to her- it does not always work well. It was the section about Abby. I think I scared her.

TURNING FORTY

Well, last night was Friday the thirteenth, and it was a full moon besides. I met Mucci and Jay, and we had dinner on Sunset.

I had one of those dreams last night that awakens one with a sense of panic that takes hours to shake off. I was in Bayside at the house, and I was floating around in space. There were these Mexicans at my parents' house, and I saw my grandmother. I floated in and out of the house. I also saw Erin, a friend of mine. I floated onto the second floor and into the bathroom. A special type of showerhead was installed, but it did not function very well. I wanted to take a shower. I took off my hat, and part of my head was shaved, and the other part had hair on it. I was upset and started to scream at everyone. I didn't want them to remove anything, and I grabbed at a lighting fixture. I sat on the floor of the bathroom and then cried. That was a heavy dream. I sat on my bed afterwards and was unable to fall back asleep. That was how my Monday, October 17, 2000, started. Welcome to my life.

The drive to Venice was long and dangerous. I had to navigate Hollywood, East LA and West LA all in the same morning, which really sucked and always left me in a very phrenetic mood in the morning.

My class on Borderlines had some very unusual and bizarre characters. I mean, it is a class on borderlines. I think it brings them all out, and that includes me, although I wouldn't say that I am a borderline, but rather that I enjoy some borderline characteristics. Lisa was in her mark with all of her stories, and we all loved it. It was story time in class, and we all gathered around.

On Friday, instead of the Sunset Strip, we all met at the Four Seasons hotel. Soft classical music played as the clatter of crystal glasses could be heard in the background. Cute girls sat at the table on the left. Occasionally, they turned, looked, and smiled. This was not the right place to bring out a laptop, but I felt compelled to do so nonetheless. I hated to stop. I am addicted.

Then the drinks and snacks arrived. They serve olives, roasted almonds, and some spicy little pea-shaped crackers, along with nice snacks.

I munched on the olives as the guests strolled on the oriental rugs. The room was fifty by fifty square. The walls were covered with art and mirrors. The painting to my left was of a chimp in a black and white block print, which was very odd but artistic.

This hotel serves as a gateway for travel around the world. Celebrities loomed around. There were fragrant, beautiful white orchid centerpieces on the table, a nice touch.

I thought about the blind date I had for lunch. She was not too bad, except for that little mole between her eyes. We talked about everything and got along well. The blind date and I met at Chaya Venice, a local culinary standout in Venice. When the eighty-dollar lunch was over, yes, that's right, I honestly spent eighty on lunch. Pretty stupid. I walked her to her car. There in plain view was a ticket on the window, and it was only thirty-five dollars. I offered to pay, but she refused. Now that is rare. I told her I was a millionaire; I love to say that. We argued about the ticket for ten minutes; it was the best part of the date. "No, give me back the ticket. No way, I'll pay for it; it's my treat. Give me back the ticket." "You get the next one." "Come on, you got lunch." "Don't worry, I'm a millionaire." "If you're a millionaire, just write me a check." She insisted, so I finally gave it back to her.

The new job took a turn for the worse today. Our supreme leader has requested that we sign in and out from now on. We had to write down the exact minute; this drove me crazy.

It was very unnerving. It is a bad omen. It reminded me that I was in prison. I began to think of getting the resume ready to go.

Back in the Four Seasons, Mucci and Jay arrived a few minutes later, and we sat and ate smoked almonds like millionaires. Never move once you have a seat, I always say, but Mucci saw some ladies in the other room—the one with the bar in it—so we moved into the Main room. A few minutes after we sat down, James Caan walked by us. He did not say hello. The bar was filled with the usual Four Seasons crowd: out-of-towners, local middle class, and a few girls who looked like they were working hard, and of course, some undercover millionaires. There was no way I could get a rap while sitting down, but we just waited there. I must have had a few pounds of almonds and dozens of olives. Mucci pitched his jazz cartoon to me, and I threw him "The Meter Maid," a very Hollywood moment.

In the room we were in, initially, a table of the most beautiful women appeared; remember…never change your seat unless it is a sure thing or an outstanding possibility. The Four Seasons was now classified as an HBC (high babe count). These women must have been playmates or something, and for the next hour, we tried to figure out how to get the table next to them, but the two guys sitting there had no intention of leaving. Are you crazy?

It's Friday night, and it's the Friday before Halloween. There is an art show downtown at the place where I exhibited my baby, the shark. I was told that it was a black-tie affair and that I could come after the initial crowd had settled in. I walked in all black and was pretty wasted. I could see that the party was well under way. There was red wine being served, so I wandered over there and ordered a glass. I offered to pay as Charles walked over to me and said that all that had been taken care of.

Charles asked me who I was; well, actually, he said, "You must be an artist." "That's right," and I proudly pointed to my painting. I was carrying a blue bag on my side, and the weight was causing me to lean from side to side. Several women were walking around, examining the art. They were wearing gowns and short, tight black skirts. I was the artist in the show, so I began to flirt, I mean, that's my job.

I met a wonderful woman from Georgia, and she was as you'd expect: sweet, and as a bonus, she was a nurse. Her tall, curvaceous body turned heads immediately, and I could hardly resist the temptation. So, I started to talk with Autumn. I followed her around all evening. She was charming, and at the end of the evening, she was one of three numbers that I collected.

Bush won the election. This does not seem to be good news to most of the population in California. Fuck... Bush is president. I think it is time to build a bomb shelter because if my predictions are correct, then this is the beginning of the end. That is right: World War III. Ok... I said it, but I didn't think it could happen. Well, wake up and smell the coffee. Nostradamus predicted that the village idiot would rule the new world, and well... who wants to argue with him? I am sure the election will go down as one of the closest in a long time. Father and son. That's a tough team to beat. Bush, it is going to be one of those years.

The election continued for a long time as the votes were carefully counted. It was all over the news: the butterfly ballot. I stayed out of it. We were all in suspense, but the courts took their time, and the entire world waited. Gore won the popular vote but lost the state in the Electoral College. How fucked is that?

It's Sunday, and I was playing the role of "Sunday therapist" today. The morning was more leisurely; I did not have to be there until ten am for my client. Supervision was cake. The supervisor saved me for last, and then there wasn't much time left. We discussed one client and her relationship with her cat. The cat is a metaphor. She told me that she was thinking of putting the cat to sleep; she said it was old, but we had our doubts. The cat then escaped from the house. What does that mean? Is that a part of her unconscious that she wants to set free? She likes kittens but hates the older cat. Now that sounds like a fear of death to me. The older part represents that part of her that is dying, decaying. By getting rid of it, she extends her aging and therefore her death. Extremely basic, I think I didn't say any of this to her, but it was very fertile ground at supervision.

I got to take two naps at the clinic, although the second one was interrupted by an alarm going off on the phone. It seems that one of the therapists was locked in the room. She tried to open the door to throw some parents out, and the doorknob came off in her hand. Now that must have been impressive.

But my favorite for the day was the last couple. They were in their forties, black, and struggling with a new boy. The two parents had a history of drugs. The boy crawled around on the floor as they complained about a lack of trust. We must let go of the history a little. Pat, the boyfriend, stared into space as only a former junkie could, his eyes black and lifeless. "I love her," he declared. "I want a family; I want to be together with her, but this shit about this other guy at my place giving her massages…that's bullshit." "You weren't there… how do you think I felt?" He screamed at his girlfriend; the girl had an attraction for speed and other things that supported her craziness. The two of them had families with plenty of drugs and alcohol in their history, and they were struggling to be free. Sam, the boy, crawled into the pile of pillows. "It's our first time in therapy; she thought that it was hard for me." For me? It is easy; I thought to myself, for the two of you, that's what is going to be hard. They both said they loved each other. But I could tell that the girlfriend wasn't as codependent as the boyfriend. She was already planting the "even if we aren't together line." When the clinic director heard about the case, I was immediately taken off the case. Couples, shit. What the fuck do I know? I have not had a good relationship in years, if ever. I mean, I am a bachelor millionaire—emphasis on bachelor's.

Chapter 21 The Clinic

I heard a lot about addictions today. Either they're clean and sober, or they're trying to be. Boy, after a day like this, I never want to do any drugs again, and let that be a lesson to you all. It's incredible how much drugs have become a part of everyone's history. The self-soothing aspect of drugs is needed to counter the pain of the fear of death, which is very existential.

By early morning, I had received a call from the clinic director, who informed me that I had been grossly inappropriate in allowing the couple to come in. Oh no. They wanted to talk, and I let them talk. Big deal. Where has our humanity gone? She said it was sweet. How nice of her. She is lucky we don't have elections here.

I spoke to my mom later in the day. We always talk at the same time: five thirty on the East Coast, right after dinner for her. It pains me that there is not more I can do for her. I try to call her every day. What do we talk about? How's work?" she asks. She then asks me about my father, "How is he?" she wants to know. "He died four years ago." "Did we get a stone?" "Yes,

Mom. We took care of it." What did he die from? "Mom, we were there. He had a stroke. It was peaceful." "Did we get a stone?" "Yes, we got a stone, and we said a prayer for him. Don't you remember?" "No," she replies, "Oh, that is OK. We took care of it. Do not worry." Is she worried about her death? Is that why she asks so many questions? I go through the same set of questions every time I call. I try to be there for her and help her laugh a little. There isn't much to joke about, but I try.

She asks about my job. Does she know what I am doing? I tell her I am a few blocks from the beach, and the job is fine. Sometimes she asks about school. It's all okay, because that's how it is.

My father died four years ago today. I have not talked about him much, but I think of him often. Fathers and Sons; that is a whole topic. He was my Aunt Lilly's brother. I was with him when he died. I was holding his hand. He had short, pudgy fingers. It was one of those unforgettable and beautiful experiences that life has to offer. I did not know what to do. The stroke left him on life support. There were tubes and wires. He could not see me, even though his eyes were wide open. I tried all my magic, and I could not bring him back. My mom and I pondered what to do. He was in the hospital for two months. He looked terrible.

We should have let him live, but was he alive? I do not know. The first time my mom and I looked at him to turn off the machines, she couldn't do it. I didn't know what to do, so we left and discussed things. I was having an out-of-body experience. How strange it all seems now, yet it felt like the beginning of the end of my family as I knew it. How did he die? He should have lived many more years, but the family stress ultimately took its toll on him. He was only seventy-three. That seems young. I wanted to say goodbye to him again. Our last conversation was about borrowing money. I did not know what he was up to, and he was very private. He had plenty of money. So, what did he need the money for? I was broken at the time and had no credit cards; I should have offered to help. Who knew it was to be the last conversation? Sometimes, life sucks like that, and there was nothing I could do. Think about it, that each conversation might be the last. Remember always to conclude a discussion on a positive note.

The clock in my living room is now one hour ahead. I just left it because of the change to daylight saving time. So, when I'm in the living room, it always seems later than when I walk into the bedroom. I might make it six hours ahead and make it confusing.

I got a new car. It is a Chevy Blazer. I suppose that when you're about to turn forty, you start to think about safety and storage more than when you're younger. I wanted that red Ferrari 400i, a twelve-cylinder. That looked amazing and practical. It had four seats. But in the end, I got the Blazer. Fuck, how domestic I have become.

Last night was Saturday night, and I needed some action. I dislike the fact that since I work at the clinic on Sundays, I have to take it easy on Saturday nights. I am a little upset as well, since Melinda, the girl with the mole between her eyes, called me on Friday to let me know that she was seriously dating another guy. Was she kidding? I had gone out with her twice. Okay, it's not a lot, but still, we've talked numerous times on the phone. In any case, she called me and provided me with that new piece of information. I was very annoyed, but I tried to remain as positive as possible. Then, she asked me if I wanted to meet a friend of hers, a nice Peruvian girl. I said that's okay, I'll pass and have a good life, and maybe someday we can all get together. Yea right, fuck you too.

TURNING FORTY

So, Saturday came, and it had been six months at least since my last sexcapade. I had that hungry look, and it was starting to get on my nerves. It had been a long time since the strip club, so I figured, why not? At first, I went to the one on Sunset, but I don't know; it wasn't as familiar as the one on La Cienega. So, after paying the entrance fee and an additional ten dollars for water, I left Sunset for La Cienega. Did you get that one? Ten dollars for water, nice huh?

The strip club was already chock-full by the time I arrived, and so I sat down quietly. This time, I ordered a couple of ten-dollar fake beers and watched as the clothes started to come off. I recognized some of the girls, and as usual, there were some new ones. After spending a few dollars here and there, I decided to sit on the side and watch the action from the sidelines. It's a little less intimidating, and the girls will come and sit down beside you.

So, after sitting for a while, Sasha sat down and grabbed my arm, and in a beautiful Russian accent, asked me if I wanted a lap dance. At first, I said no, but then we discussed various things and talked it over. She said she was studying international economics. "Not bad for a stripper," I thought. She also added that she was alone. Perhaps she chopped up her ex. I am sometimes surprised at the things that strippers say, and this was one of them. She told me she was an only child and that she loved to travel. She had a fantastic body with beautiful breasts and a big smile, with small teeth. She was so cute that I could sit there for hours talking to her. Occasionally, she would ask me if I wanted a lap dance, and I would say, "Not right now," and we would continue our conversation.

I knew that I was going to get a lap dance, but I had to wait 'til I was ready. I have only had two other lap dances in my life, and neither was very exciting, so I didn't feel the need to rush into it. She got up to do a regular dance, and she danced in a way that was very different from everyone else. She had strong, bold moves, distinct from the others, and yet she was very sexy, and the men watched with their mouths open as I did.

The evening continued, and it was getting late. It was now or never, and I must admit that I was terrified. But it was late, and if I were going to get one, now would be the time. I asked her, "How about that dance?" and we walked into the back room and the little booth. At first, it seemed slow, and then she picked up the pace. She went up and down on my body, forward and backward. She took off her bra, and her beautiful body was in my face. I touched her breast ever so carefully, and then her waist, and I was getting very turned on.

The music was blasting. Every few minutes, the guard would check on us, so I would move my hands away from touching her body, and then he would leave, and I would start again. This went on and on. At one point, after the third song, I made a move and pulled a muscle on my right side. It felt like a heart attack. What a way to go. She kept pumping and rubbing, and suddenly, I came. Oh my, I had an orgasm. That was amazing. I clutched her body the way one does. Now that was a lap dance.

I started to pay her, shaking ever so slightly from the intensity of the experience. How much do I owe her? Was that a long dance? I started taking out twenties, and then she said that was six dances. "Six? Ok… well, how much do I owe you?" I was scared to ask. At this point, money was no object. "That's one hundred and eighty," she said. I could only smile inside… sounds reasonable to me. "I just need to go to the ATM," which was conveniently located inside the club. I gave her two hundred forty, which seemed right to me in the moment, and smiled. Now that was a Saturday night, ne pas?

We sat down. She kept saying, "Wait there, and I'll be back." She had been wearing her usual black lace hot pants.

I told her I would like to take her out to dinner. "OK," she said, "tomorrow night." Tomorrow night? I thought to myself, that is, after working 9 hours at the clinic. Well, as if I could say no. "All right. Let me get your number." I scrambled for a pen, the most essential ingredient for the single man. No pens, shit. OK. "Don't worry, I'll be there." OK, whatever, a date with a full nude stripper from Russia, are you crazy? When will that ever happen again? She was amazing with those big green eyes. Not to mention the pinkish satin bra. That is it—no special elaborate outfit, just the minimalist.

"Where are we going to meet?" "How about at Sunset Plaza's parking lot?" That made me nervous, I mean, she's KGB and I'm going to be kidnapped by a beautiful Russian spy. It could happen, I mean, it happens to James Bond all the time. I immediately started thinking that I should tell someone where I would be, just in case. So, we debate locations for a while, and then we agree to meet at Chin Chin's on Sunset. That is always a well-lit location with parking.

I waited and waited. Okay, I was early, but that's fine. Then, suddenly, I could see her from about fifty feet. She was wearing a black leather jacket and silver metallic shoes with short, transparent stockings. Wow, that's a dream. Humna, humna, as Jackie would say. We shared a brief hug and a kiss on the cheek. It was a moment. Her thick Russian accent required me to focus with superhuman concentration so as not to lose track of what she was saying.

Where to go on a date with a stripper in LA? Since we were already on Sunset, that was going to be our main course of action. And besides, who cares? Any small romantic spot will do. So, we walked across the street to this Italian restaurant. Before

I left, I had eaten two bananas just in case. You know, for potassium. So, I was not that hungry, but she was, of course. We ordered the mozzarella pesto appetizer. I was amazed that LA women would have the nerve to order that and still feel good about themselves. She did, and she was proud. I let her take charge. The woman came by with the wine list. Sasha went over it carefully but could not decide. She went back and forth, debating between Merlot and Chianti—such tough decisions. I just sat back, and we finally agreed on something. Who cares? She will drink me under the table anyway.

What was she like? She was taking an American constitutional law class at some local LA school and busting her ass doing so. I was amazed. She explained it all to me in that sexy Russian accent. I told her my favorite food story. It's always a hit; the audience always laughs. It goes like this… I once attended a business lunch meeting, where I ordered sea bass at the company's expense. The waiter came over to the table, and I mistakenly heard, "Would you like me to flavor this for you? " Instead of " filet. " So, I started to think about chocolate? But that seemed strange. Instead, he was asking if I wanted him to fillet it, fillet it, I heard flavor it." She laughed a little. Shit, my best stories weren't working. This could be a long evening.

The evening went on as she sucked down her trout covered in cream sauce, and I snacked on my sea bass. She was an Aries, she told me. We drank a bottle of wine, of course. "Would you like some dessert?" the server asked. "No," she said, "I never drink coffee. I will have a Remy Martin cognac." Damn, a cognac, and now I'm really in trouble. Ok, well, here we go, a little hardball. Straight up, of course, no ice.

Then we went for a walk down Sunset. It was one of those beautiful evenings. She kept saying I was so intellectual. She even showed me her license, although I must admit I was pretty drunk by then from the wine and cognac. I never showed her mine. It was a warm night, and the air had that great hot winter feeling. I gently put my hand on her back for a moment.

We went over to the Standard, a hotel on Sunset. There was a pool outside. I figured we could go for a swim. We sat at the table and ordered; that's right, some more Remy Martins. They're only about $12 each, which is very reasonable. I slowly ran my hands through her hair. I rubbed her temples and slowly ran my hands over her metallic shoes, which rested on my knees. The stars were out. I pointed out the seven sisters, Venus, and Mars. "Isn't that red?" I asked her. She agreed. She loved all that intellectual stuff and cash. So I sprouted as many intellectual moments as I could and paid all the bills. It was beautiful outside, and we just sat by the pool.

It was all very calm considering that Don Juan was sitting with a Russian stripper. But, like any good Don knows, patience is the key to getting laid, and besides, she was tough, in a sexy way. So, I settled for just rubbing all over her body except for the good parts. It was a first date, and I still didn't have her number. I walked her to her car. A brand-new Cadillac. She told me she did not know how to drive when she got it. I asked her for a ride to my new Blazer. I was proud.

Inside the car, everything was in order. We did not make out or anything. So, I got her number and wrote it down on the back of a slip of paper, and then I stumbled back to my car. I felt pretty good considering how much I had to drink. But I got into the car like a good fool and took off.

I tried to catch up with her in the Cadillac and almost did, except that I somehow ended up taking a shortcut at a slightly higher speed. I not only caught up with her, but the LAPD caught up to me. That's right, I was being followed by a black and white. "Ok… must remain calm," I keep telling myself. I see them through the back of the Blazer. I have had the

145

car for exactly one day. Am I crazy? Will I have to give up this car one day? I see Wilton Ave coming up, so I make a right turn. They haven't flashed me. I should realize that they will follow me. I must risk it. They won't. Not this time. They have not put on their lights yet. So, I go halfway down the street and pull over. The police officers stop alongside me and flash their floodlights on my window, which I roll down. "Going a little fast, what's going on?" "Oh, I was just trying to catch up with my girlfriend." "Really? Fight?" "No, just a date." That was a stupid thing to say, I think to myself. Whatever. "Do you live here? No, just visiting a friend of mine." "Ok," they say. "Thank you for wearing your seatbelt," and they take off—a beat. Thank you, thank you. I sit in the car and watch them drive away. Can you believe that four glasses of red wine and two glasses of Remy Martin, and they slowly drive away. How lucky is that?

The boss is out, so I take a momentary break from the daily grind and spend most of the day attending to life's tasks and shuffling papers.

When I get home that night, I want to call her, but I cannot find the slip of paper with her number on it, and I start to panic. We agreed to go out on Friday, and I'm not going to miss it.

Where is the slip of paper? I go through everything twice, and still I cannot find it. I get more nervous. Did I leave it at the office? There is only one thing to do. Call the strip club and see if she is working tonight. I could have just asked for her on the phone, but I decided to go down and get it from her in person. Not my original plan for the evening, but whatever. So I drive to the club, but first I go to the ATM and remove a C note. I mean, I am going to the strip club.

When I arrived, Sasha was speaking with the owners. I am sure she was talking to them about something. She gave me a big smile and a hello peck, and we sat over by the couch. It was romantic. We talked for a while, and then I asked her for her number again. I was a little embarrassed and wasn't sure exactly what to say, other than that I wanted it, which is why I came here. She smiled with her cute little teeth and big green eyes, and then she asked me if I wanted a dance. Shit, what kind of dance? "You know." Oh no, not another 195. I could get it for free, and somehow, I said yes.

So, we went back again. I wasn't that into it and wasn't entirely sure how to say no, at least the second time. I think I have learned by now. In any case, there I was in the back with her, gyrating in her usual Russian manner.

I was starting to get into it, but three songs had already been played: that's ninety. I asked to stop, and believe me, that was a tough decision. That was a mere nine minutes. But I was thinking I was Rockefeller, so I slowly stood and paid. We walked out together and sat down on the spot where we had been before. We began having casual conversations about schools. I was telling her about psychology, and I think she was getting a little turned on. I knew I was in rare form when I heard myself saying "quantitative analytic chemistry" to her. Yes, we had to weigh each crucible four times. Then the dreaded thing happened: her name was called. It was time for her to dance. "Do you want to see?" she asked. "OK," and I walked over to the dance pit.

There was a group of guys. It was, after all, a Monday night, and there were three groups of two, as I could tell. The woman DJ bantered in the back. "Tip generously, she needs to pay her bills." Then the music started, and Sasha began her gyrations. Her tall, strong body was like a statue on the stage, and everyone watched. She shook, bent, and slipped out of her pink satin bra. The guys started to shout at her. "How much are your bills?" They threw money at her. I placed the rest of my cash on the counter. It was all hard to watch. She kept smiling, but I could tell she was pissed and would have loved to kick them with her plastic stiletto shoes. She went on, and one balding guy kept saying, "Next." That was hard. Poor Sasha. It was over, and she walked off the stage with her hips swinging, her chin in the air, taking a deep breath.

We sat for a moment, and then I told her I needed to go. "I'll call you. I have your number." It only cost me a little over $100 to get it. I didn't say that to her. Am I crazy or what? When I arrived at work the next day, her number was still correct, where I had left it on the desk.

My mom said to me that she wasn't hysterical. I said, "It's good you're not hysterical," and then she started to laugh. Yeah, it's good—the sweet sound of laughter.

Sasha and I planned a date together. Maybe we can go to the beach. She had talked about how much she loved the beach. I, of course, was in complete agreement with her. Initially, we agreed on noon, but then she changed it to an earlier time. I, of course, was still convinced that I was to be kidnapped by the KGB, but I kept that to myself. I told her I would pick her up. I didn't know where I was going, but I realized I needed cash. I'm sure I could have taken out three hundred, but I started with a hundred and figured I could sign for the rest. The Friday after Thanksgiving is usually a very restful day, but I knew it was going to be something very different. Sasha was wearing a dark black velvet turtleneck, making her somewhat invincible against my warm, empathic hands. She was also wearing those silver shoes with tight black stretch pants. Not bad, huh? Then add a very soft black leather Harley-Davidson jacket, and you have the perfect outfit. Well, she was all in black, the color of LA fashion.

What music should I play? I went through the limited collection I had in the car and threw on a new Enya CD. Mellow, it will show the sensual side of me. Sasha didn't care. I think she was finally happy to be going somewhere without having to drive herself. I was so excited I could hardly keep my hands off her.

We decided to go to Santa Barbara, a pleasant day trip with a stripper.

Sasha and I wandered around the town drinking cognac and taking deep breaths of the good air. At one point, we lay down on the grass and paused for a moment. I can't remember what I said, but it seemed all very superficial. She was friendly but distant, and after a few hours and a hundred-dollar brunch, we headed back to LA.

We went back to her place, so I naturally thought something good was about to happen. Sasha had a dog I found, a dog that must have been trained as a watchdog. The moment I got into her place, the dog began his tricks. It was no use; Bugsy got all the action. So after about an hour of frustration, I left.

"It's not easy money, but it's fast," Sasha would say. But tonight, it didn't seem that fast. I visited her at the club along with all the other girls. It must have been a tranquil Monday night since all the girls looked bored. I sat down next to Sasha. There was another woman between us, and this was to be the metaphor for the evening. She looked perfect in her pink satin bra, and I, as usual, had a hard time concentrating on talking with her. After a while, she asked if I wanted a dance. When I said no, she told me that this other guy wanted one and walked across the room to the other side, starting to work on him. I wasn't that upset, after all; we talked every day, but that was it, and it was never a very sexy conversation.

So, she went over and worked on her next dance, and I sat there watching all the action. One by one, they came up to me and asked if I wanted a lap dance. I kept saying no, and then Iris sat down next to me. We talked for the first time in a long time, and she told me that she enjoys gardening. She grew plants and flowers, and it seemed to bring her joy. I told her that I had put her in my book, and I recited a short paragraph. Something like, "Iris would lean over and brush her soft, sweet-smelling hair against me, and for a moment I was in heaven, all else faded away, all I could think of was Iris, and then I was back." She laughed; it was a moment of humor. Then Cynthia came over and sat down next to me. She was terrific, with one of those petite bodies and sexy eyes that made me dream of another life with her. Cynthia complained about her boring summer, saying she hadn't done anything exciting. I had fantasies about our summer together, but a few minutes later, she added that she got bored when she wasn't giving a lap dance. Marketing; it's always about marketing. She said that she was going to get some junk food.

Sasha walked over to me and sat down. It was getting late, and it was about time to leave. She asked if I wanted a lap dance. I remember the last one that cost over a hundred and said no. She was surprised and started to ask me, "Why not?" in that broken Russian accent. "I'm tired." She was annoyed and kept asking me, "Why not?" I had nothing left to say, so I told her I was going to leave. She was pissed. But who cares, I mean, why spend all that money? I got in my car and was on my way.

Chapter 22 Basketball

I now realize that I am getting too old for basketball. I was reminded of that today. I played two full-court games, making about seven three-pointers. I wish I could say that I was good. But I was at least able to keep up.

What did my mom say when I called her on December 25, 2000?

TURNING FORTY

Did Dad die?

Where was the funeral?

Did you have it done by Glassman?

Did you get a special?

Jim

Uncle Sam, mother's brother…

What kind of stroke?

He's buried?

How many people were there?

Was I there?

If I were there.

If he were a mensch, he wouldn't have died…

It was always heavy, and I never knew what to say.

I just came from a massage and a deep healing session. It seems that all we store within our muscles. These memories remain with us for a long time. Who knows how long? Of course, it's hard to release things. The first part of the massage covered the various areas of my body. Isn't everything sensitive at some point? Then it went further, deep into the tissues and muscles. Suddenly, I started to flash through many different memories of all the injuries that I have had. She hit a particular sore spot under my left shoulder. That was it. That was the center of some deep-rooted fear, death anxiety. It went deeper and deeper. My childhood flashed before me. Then I started to recall my father tapping me on the shoulder. Wow, that is a physical memory too, in my tissues. I had to pause and think about that. It had been a long time since I had felt my father's touch.

And speaking about touch, I had an awe-inspiring night last night. It was Friday night. I had a date. Imagine that. It was an old friend. I met Chloe four years ago at an art show. Nothing had happened back then, but I wanted to remain optimistic. We had been exchanging emails, and recently she began signing them, "Love Chloe," so I was confident for a good reason. I set the time for 8:00 p.m. on Friday. She was late, but that's how I remember her being the last time we got together. She was driving her mother's car. She couldn't find her keys.

When she stepped out, I noticed she had brought a bottle of red wine and a bag. I was a little surprised. I mean, I can't remember the last time a woman brought me a bottle of wine. She was also carrying another bag. I was to find out what that was later.

Chloe was wearing a beige coat with a fur collar. I'm sure if the people in PETA saw this, she would have been in trouble. But that never came up in conversation. She came in and perused the mess that I called home, and I walked into the kitchen to wash out two glasses. "Pretty bad, huh? No clean glasses." I opened the wine, and then we sat down on the couch and had a toast. "What is in the bag?" I thought.

There was a massive surprise in the bag. It was her art slides. I had remembered saying "bring the slides," but who knew? I didn't have a slide projector, so I had to rely on my halogen lights. I looked at the first slide and was very glad that I had asked her to bring them along. Chloe was now into photography or at least posing in lingerie. Slide after slide, she was wearing white slips and black lace. I had to examine each one closely. Was she not wearing underwear? I guess not. I looked at the slide and then looked back at her. Her slender 27-year-old body was the only thing on my mind, and I slowly reached over and put my hand on the back of her neck. She cooed, and then I ran my hands through her hair. Then I went back and looked at more slides; there were plenty to look at: dozens and dozens. I was getting very turned on. Could this be happening to me? She kept smiling and laughing as she handed me the slides. I was a little nervous. She downed her glass of wine in one gulp. Shit, I was in trouble.

We talked about art. I walked her over to the corner of the room to show her the painting I had made for my class on borderlines. Somewhere between explaining the colors and the meaning, we started to make out. I ran my hands over her body repeatedly. It had been a long time. We stood next to that painting for ten minutes and then moved into the bedroom.

I unbuttoned her clothes. We fell into my bed and didn't get up 'til the morning. Her warm body was next to mine, and that felt great. Sex at night. Have sex when you wake up. That's what life is about. I stopped for a moment of reflection and looked at the calendar. I realized that tomorrow is my birthday, and guess what? I'm Turning Forty.

The End.

###

Mitch Rubman Education

TURNING FORTY

Master's degree, Antioch University; attended NYU Graduate School of Journalism, Boston University BA, Planetary and Space Sciences—Bronx High School of Science.

www.ingramcontent.com/pod-product-compliance
Lightning Source LLC
Chambersburg PA
CBHW050131280326
41933CB00010B/1327